Strange
SOMERSET
Stories

Introduced by David Foot

Bossiney Books

First published in 1984
by Bossiney Books
St Teath, Bodmin, Cornwall
Designed, typeset and printed in Great Britain by
Penwell Ltd, Parkwood, Callington
Cornwall

© *Ray Waddon, Jack Hurley*
Hilary Wreford, David Foot
Lornie Leete-Hodge, Rosemary Clinch
Michael Williams 1984

ISBN O 906456 87 8

PLATE ACKNOWLEDGMENTS

Front cover by Mark Bygraves
Pages 5-7, 16, 17, 22, 40, 66-9, 72, 82, 86, 89, 91, 92, 97,
102, back cover Julia Davey
Pages 9, 33, 37 Michael Deering
Pages 10, 15 Ray Waddon
Pages 13, 27, 49, 70, 74, 94 Paul Honeywill
Pages 28, 55-9 Bryan Russell
Pages 43, 44, 47, 76 Felicity Young
Page 50 M. Tarr
Page 51 Somerset County Cricket Club
Page 84 Christopher Trubridge
Page 87 Rosemary Clinch

Contents

Introduction

DAVID FOOT

Perhaps it isn't at all a bad thing for a cynical old professional journalist like myself to write the introduction to a book of this nature. The captive collaborator is usually easy to find. But there is a tendency, then, for the words to sound glib and exaggerated. Credibility can suffer in the process.

Michael Williams, that most prolific and proficient of 'cottage' publishers is of course an old hand at strange stories. Long ago he discovered that life was full of imponderables. He had a healthy interest in the Occult and he researched—whenever he could find a little spare time from his busy publishing activities—with diligence and passion. And, he would assure you, with an open mind.

Certainly not all the stories in this present collection are about the Occult. Most of them carry a twist or a question mark—and in their different ways are of absorbing interest, not simply to readers who belong to the region which is the location for these tales. This is not a book of fiction. Bizarre it may have been, but there really was an Abode of Love at Spaxton, as a few of the tabloids like titillatingly to remind us on various anniversaries. The extraordinary child murder happened on Exmoor, just as Jack Hurley tells us.

It is probably an appropriate moment to write of Jack Hurley, too. For some years, he was the editor of the West Somerset Free Press. He was a distinguished provincial journalist, a reservoir of local knowledge and an acknowledged authority on Somerset folklore. He could enthral his friends—most of them his readers—with stories that swept marvellously across the wide, handsome terrain of Exmoor and the Quantocks. Jack, a gentle man with a

A brook at Sedgemoor: 'Somerset is saturated with strange stories.' ▶

rich mind, would talk about John Ridd and the Doones in one breath
—and about Somerset's greatest native cricketer, Harold Gimblett,
with whom he once attended school at Williton, in the next. Sadly,
Mr Hurley, journalist and storyteller, has now died. I imagine that
his fascinating chapter in this book was his last published work.

Every one of these Strange Somerset Stories is undeniably off-
beat. In their different styles, they convey a gripping and often eerie
atmosphere. Many of them leave questions unanswered. One or two
of them raise the hairs on the back of your neck. Above all, the
publisher has set out to intrigue his readers: to give them a racy
narrative and an evocative read. Long ago, he discovered that the
South West was fertile with legend. As a junior reporter, too, on a
weekly paper years ago I appeared to unearth an incredible claim of
the past in nearly every village.

You don't have to believe every single claim and puzzling incident
in this book, although I have a suspicion that Mr Williams does. It
is more an invitation to read—and then ponder. And it should be

Somerset's 'beautiful and varied landscape'.

remembered that a great deal has been authenticated. There are accounts of factual sightings of unexplained objects in the sky by Rosemary Clinch. A policeman's widow really was told by her late husband that he had dreamt he was going to be attacked by gipsies.

There's plenty of diversity. I grew up eavesdropping on whispered versions of what supposedly went on in the Abode of Love. No Westcountry writer was closer, geographically and journalistically, than Ray Waddon. I can't wait to read what he has to say about it. Nor about the interview, in another chapter, with a lady who makes the grandiose claim that she was Arthur in an earlier life. Another established author, Lornie Leete-Hodge tells us about some of Somerset's many hauntings; and we can hear from Hilary Wreford about a number of the curiosities to be found across the county's beautiful and varied landscape.

I am tempted to be personal and to explain why I have chosen to write of a police constable's murder well over a hundred years ago. I grew up in T.S. Eliot's lovely village of East Coker, where for years my father was the local sexton. One of his evening chores was manually to wind the old clock and chimes. Occasionally, I did it for him—and on a winter's evening, carrying only a flickering lantern, a deserted church could be incredibly spooky.

For a reason I could never explain, one leaning tombstone a few yards in from the iron gate of the church path always frightened me. In the bible-blackness of the night, that particular tombstone for ever reminded me of a stooping, old man. I'd catch my schoolboy's breath and hurry up the spiral staircase to the clocktower. And because I was cursed with an unrelenting imagination, I made sure the lantern was placed near the doorway so that I could keep a wary eye on the stairs as I wound the chimes.

No distorted figure from the supernatural ever appeared, though each creak or crumble of plaster from this old Norman church was magnified to fearful proportions. When I grew older and less susceptible, I paused one sunny afternoon to read the inscription on the leaning tombstone. It told me that PC Nathaniel Cox had been killed in the discharge of his duty. That was later to generate my own researches. Cox was murdered—even if manslaughter was the official verdict—in 1876. Parishioners at East Coker still talk of it. The names of the poachers involved are still mentioned with the kind of scorn directed at them at the time of the infamous and much publicised court case.

'. . . the wide handsome terrain of Exmoor.'

The point is that Constable Cox's tombstone, of all those in that churchyard, terrified me BEFORE I learned of the circumstances of the policeman's gory death. Years later I exorcised those erstwhile fears of childhood and capitalised on the macabre ramblings of my imagination. I used that same grey, creepy tombstone in my first published short story—and, of course, I allowed a figure from the past to appear in the dim lit doorway of the clock tower. I was paid two guineas for the story.

Over recent years the publisher has brought out *Strange Happenings in Cornwall* and *Strange Stories from Devon.* Both apparently found a ready readership. Now it is the turn of Somerset. He told me: 'I think that Somerset in particular is, like Cornwall, saturated with strange stories. Maybe it is because there were until recently largely isolated areas in both. As a Cornishman, it's fact that I have always felt closer to Cornwall in Somerset than in Devon —and something deeper than an Arthurian thing. Anyway I'm sure we have only scratched the surface. There are many more odd stories to tell.'

Legend is one thing. Superstitions are another. Add them to the distinctive regional characteristics evolved over many centuries. I still remember an old countryman who used to suck his gnarled pipe and lean over his gate to talk to me as a small boy. He'd tell me stories, passed down to him by his grandfather, and he swore they were all factual.

'Ah, 'twas all true, son. True as I'm hure. The best stories, the strange ones, did really happen.'

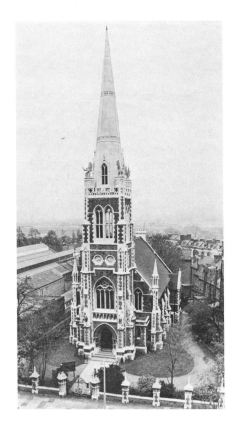

The Church of the Ark of the Covenant in Clapton, built by Brother Prince in the 1890s. In 1902 the Reverend Hugh Smyth-Pigott proclaimed himself the new Messiah.

10

The Self-Styled Messiah

RAY WADDON

After nine years in which he started as junior reporter on a weekly newspaper—long since defunct —in his native Bridgwater, Ray Waddon set up as a freelance, covering a wide variety of Somerset events for national and foreign newspapers. He specialised in Somerset customs, broadcasting before the war and later appearing on television with his personal memories.

An eerie silence followed the lusty singing of a hymn by the well-dressed congregation in the white stone church, the 'Ark of the Covenant' in the select north-east London suburb of Clapton.

One of the three beautiful stained-glass windows was suddenly darkened by a cloud on this memorable Sunday evening in early September 1902. It lent dramatic impact to an amazing pronouncement by a tall man in clerical attire.

Leading up to a semi-circular marble altar were richly carpeted steps. Beyond was a throne on which he was seated. Emaciated, of sallow countenance, he had dark glistening bright eyes. His thin black hair was parted down the centre of his small head.

Slowly he rose and stood looking fixedly at the many worshippers of both sexes. Then, speaking softly, almost musically, but with deliberation, he declared: 'I who speak to you tonight am that Lord Jesus Christ who died and rose again, and ascended into Heaven. I am that Lord Jesus, come again in my own body, to save those who come to me from death and judgment.'

The Reverend John Hugh Smyth-Pigott paused in his blasphemous staggering utterances, which were to make national and indeed, international headlines.

Gazing abstractly at his astounded hearers and raising his right hand, he said: 'It is not there, in Heaven, where you will find your God, but in me who am united with the Father.'

Slowly he walked back, sat down and buried his head in his hands. Silence again, broken this time by a woman crying: 'God is here! I see Him on the altar!'

'Behold! That is God,' said another.

A grey haired man rose, excitedly shouting: 'Behold! that is Christ!' One after another stood 'testifying to the Lord God' in emphatic penetrating tones.

The entire body joined in singing to organ accompaniment 'Oh Hail Thou King of Glory'. Exuberant women, young and old, rushed to try and touch the arch-imposter with the same fervour as present-day hysterical girls whose shrieks and screams drown the cacophony of their pop group idols.

The wide publicity given in the press throughout the week, despite failure to interview Pigott, resulted in extraordinary scenes the following Sunday. For the morning service people had begun to take up positions before the locked gate of the church by six o'clock. Eventually about two hundred were admitted.

In clerical garb, and wearing a hat, Pigott's arrival in a pair-horse brougham was the signal for hisses and booing. Inside he repeated his declaration of a week earlier that he was the new Messiah. Apart from a few interruptions the service passed off without incident.

Directly it was over there were wild and ugly scenes. By tram and brake, on cycle and on foot, an angry crowd numbering several thousand had gathered. Women moaned. Some fainted in the crush. Journalists were among the people swept aside in the mad rush. Police were unable to cope with the situation. Reinforcements arrived, many of them mounted, but faced a hard task in efforts to control the noisy mob and protect Pigott from violence.

Some of Pigott's flock tried to shield him and he was hustled into one of two waiting broughams. Fists were raised and insults hurled as, regardless of life and limb, the front driver whipped the horses into a gallop. It was little short of miraculous that Pigott reached his charming home, Cedar Lodge, by Clapton Common, unharmed.

'At midnight, in secret, he was buried in the grounds . . . upright . . . ready for the Resurrection.' ▶

12

The news in one of the national dailies of the mounted police escort to Cedar Lodge added that Pigott was going into retreat at a rural refuge in Somerset. This was the Agapemone at Spaxton, six miles from Bridgwater.

However, to trace the events which brought Pigott to Somerset and linked him with another amazingly similar eccentric, it is necessary to go back to the end of last century.

It was the Reverend Henry John Prince who had built the 'Ark of the Covenant' Church which Pigott had sensationalised. He also bought a mansion at Spaxton, naming it the 'Abode of Love' and founding a peculiar sect known as the Agapemonites.

Like Pigott, 'Brother Prince' was a Somerset man. Born at Bath he studied medicine at Guy's Hospital, London. Ironically, ill health compelled him to give it up. Instead, he devoted himself to the Church, was ordained and given a curacy at Charlynch, a lovely little stone church dating from the eleventh century on a hill top barely a mile from the Abode of Love, or Agapemone.

Prince's passion for young women was insatiable. Blasphemous ritual preceded his union with those whom he chose to gratify his sexual desires, and he was unfrocked.

In 1899, to the utter astonishment of the wealthy coterie who had firmly believed this rogue when he proclaimed his own immortality, Prince went the way of all flesh. He was eighty eight. At midnight, in secret, he was buried in the grounds. And 'upright' it was said, ready for the Resurrection.

Prince's secretary, Edwin Douglas Malcolm Hamilton, who came to live at the Abode when he was twenty six, was thought to be a likely contender for the role of the new Messiah. A tall, broad-shouldered dour Scot, he had occupied a cottage in the large and well-kept grounds. Prince's rule had been that no male member should reside in the mansion itself. Fond of reading, Hamilton, non-smoker and vegetarian, was almost a hermit. He had promised the community he would search for a new 'Heavenly Bridegroom' apparently having no desire or intention to fulfil the exalted position.

It was in Dublin that Hamilton and Pigott met, though whether by design or accident is not clear. Hamilton persuaded him to proclaim himself as the new Messiah, and sometime after the Clapton sensation, Pigott returned to his native county, this time as the Heavenly Bridegroom of the Agapemonites. He had told Hamilton to prepare a dossier of all the members, their interests and ages.

14

Left: Attending the funeral of Smyth-Pigott in 1927.

Right: The last picture of Smyth-Pigott and, above, an early picture of Sister Ruth Preece, his 'soul bride'.

15

After perusing this carefully he wrote stating there were far too many old people there. Recruits, young and attractive, must be brought in. From overseas, he suggested.

When at length Hamilton had carried out these none-too-easy instructions, Pigott's arrival at the Agapemone was heralded by the inmates being summoned to the luxuriously furnished chapel. There he once again declared himself to be the Son of Man.

Meanwhile Pigott had married. A devout member of the church, pretty auburn-haired Catherine Reynolds, fell in love with the young clergyman; she was entranced with his preaching and no doubt succumbed to his hypnotic influence.

When Pigott and his wife moved to the Agapemone, one account stated that they took with them a family friend, young vivacious Ruth Annie Preece. Another version is that suddenly, without any explanation as to how or where he found her, Pigott, who had been

Below: The Chapel at the Abode of Love as it is today.
Left: The Chapel door.

away for some time, brought the good-looking Ruth with him. But it was Ruth, and not the woman to whom he was lawfully wed, whom he installed as his Chief Soul Bride.

And although his wife, Catherine, continued living at the Agapemone, it is certain that Ruth was the mother of his children.

This immoral conduct by Pigott aroused nation-wide publicity, and the Bishop of Bath and Wells, Dr Kennion, was determined that a citation should be served on him. It was extremely difficult to present personally the necessary legal documents. Two visits by the Bishop's secretary were abortive. 'The Messiah is away,' he was told. Eventually the complaint was served on 16 December 1908, and the Consistory Court took place about a month later at Wells Cathedral.

Outlining the case against Pigott, counsel for the Bishop referred to the uproar that had occurred at Clapton in 1902. 'Ruth Annie Preece,' he said, 'appeared to have become infatuated of Smyth-Pigott. She was one of the numerous women who attended services at that conventicle, and accompanied him to the Agapemone as his "spiritual wife" whatever that may mean.'

'It is lamentable', counsel went on, 'that the defendant has been continuing the work of the notorious "Brother Prince" and converted, or continued to allow, the beautiful little hamlet of Spaxton to be a wilderness of particularly repulsive vices.'

Within a short time of the hearing, the Bishop intimated that Pigott was incapable of holding preferment in the Church on the grounds of immorality. In his absence, he was 'unfrocked'. His third child, a daughter, was born later.

It had long been said, both in Prince's day and in Pigott's, that the Agapemonites were very generous to the poor of the parish, especially at Christmas. Consequently it was not surprising when the people of Spaxton invariably declined to give any information about the Abode or its inhabitants to visiting pressmen. Offers of bribes were scorned.

Much on the same lines as his infamous predecessor, Pigott was always most careful in the choice of his female converts. That they should be of a pretty type, to satisfy his sensual demands, was coupled with their being wealthy. Their income from whatever resources they possessed, had to be pooled. This was a strict order from him, the money being necessary to maintain the remarkable building, and for him and his favoured ones to live in luxury and free

18

from any labours apart from hobbies, such as gardening, knitting, and playing croquet.

It was easy for journalists to describe the exterior of the Agapemone. Seen from a distance, it had the traditional outline of a church; but viewed at close quarters its appearance was entirely pagan.

There was a lantern tower with a lofty and delicate tapering spire. On the four top corners were almost life-sized figures of a bull, an eagle, a lion and a man—presumably representing an angel. The bull and the lion had wings, and the 'angel' knelt in a supplicating posture with one hand pointing to the sky.

Enclosed in towering walls almost as thick and high as those of a prison, the building and grounds were further safeguarded against prying eyes by massive solid oaken doors, studded with big nails. There was a resplendent lawn, well-kept and beautiful flower beds and greenhouses filled with exotic plants.

In addition to the main structure in which were twenty bedrooms, banqueting hall, private apartments, and huge stone-flagged kitchens, several cottages provided excellent accommodation for some members. One was occupied by Hamilton, and others by the domestic staff, which included sixteen chambermaids.

The population of Bridgwater in Prince's early years at Spaxton was a mere twelve thousand. It was still very much the horse and carriage age for the affluent. Whisky was eighteen shillings a gallon, best cured ham cost sevenpence a pound, and there was little in the way of entertainment.

It was therefore an exciting, and free event, when 'Brother Prince' made his occasional visits to the town, to replenish supplies. Or maybe it was a form of self-gratification that caused him to make what were termed 'triumphant entries' in great splendour. The sight of four spanking bay horses drawing his carriage, with outrider postillion, and a number of bloodhounds alongside—at night they roamed the grounds—attracted much interest among the tradesmen and pedestrians.

In striking contrast, more than half a century later, Pigott's trips into town were commonplace. A writer in a Somerset newspaper in 1924 stated: 'The three children born to Pigott by his "spiritual bride" Sister Ruth have now grown up into bonny young people. Pigott is constantly motoring in the town, where his appearance now causes no excitement or interest.'

In the late twenties it was only on rare occasions that the Agapemone figured in the news. When it did the stories were mostly inven-
ted. The sect made it a rule to refuse any interviews; they lived in
strict privacy.

Then suddenly it was front-page news again, at home and abroad.
On Monday 21 March 1927, the *Chronicle*—which itself was to die
three years later—had an exclusive story.

Banner headlines on the front page read: 'Abode of Love loses its
"Messiah". Smyth-Pigott dies at the Agapemone. His soul wives.
The Escapades of Sister Ruth.' One of the very few photographs
ever taken of Pigott was published. It was near Taunton railway
station, some twenty years earlier.

Fleet Street descended in force and the press invasion had reached
its peak on the Thursday, to cover the funeral.

At 10.30 a special squad of police, among them a number of plain
clothes officers arrived. Some were placed on duty at the main entrance to the Agapemone. Others took up positions in the lane
alongside the mansion. More were at the rear, by way of fields and
locked gates. A bloodhound joined in guarding the extensive
grounds, barking ferociously.

In a field immediately opposite, on high ground, as an enthusias-
tic young reporter on a weekly newspaper, I attempted to climb a
telegraph pole. Before I could catch even a glimpse of what was
going on inside, a burly red-faced policeman hauled me down. Just
as a personal memento I got a good snapshot with my small camera
of one party in deep mourning entering on foot. I could identify only
Pigott's family doctor and solicitor, both from Bridgwater.

To avoid breaking the law by causing an obstruction a *Daily
Mirror* photographer instructed a Bridgwater taxi driver to go very
slowly up and down the lane, repeatedly pausing by the huge doors.
They were flung open by invisible hands each time a motorcar con-
veying mourners arrived. In the same mysterious manner they
closed.

The intrepid cameraman was precariously perched on a pair of
steps, on top of the Buick taxi. 'I've to be at Aintree tomorrow, for
the Grand National,' he told me.

Spring had come to smiling Somerset. Lambs frisked and frol-
licked in the rich pasture land. The trees were beginning to unfurl
their verdant green banners. Rooks were cawing busily about their
nests.

The lane was now devoid of traffic. We of the press contingent agreed to maintain silence as we leant against the wall nearest the chapel. Floating across in the breeze the faint strains of the organ were an indication that the burial service was taking place; but in secrecy comparable with the forbidden Tibetan city of Lhasa. So the army of newspapermen and women could describe only the general scene, and resort to letting their pens run riot in highly coloured accounts.

'A time to be born and a time to die,' says Ecclesiastes. The mortal remains of Spaxton's second self-acclaimed Messiah lay in a village-made coffin, covered by the rich red soil of the Quantock Hills country.

Would it mean that the curtain was now being run down for ever at the peaceful home of this declining and ageing sect? Occasionally if some new angle could be found they would be revived in the cold print of the more sensation-loving Sunday newspapers.

Sister Ruth, who had changed her name to Smyth, was understood to be the principal. Hamilton apparently had no desire to become the new leader.

One event in 1936 was productive of an item that served an opportunity of rehashing some of the history of the place. This was the death, and secret burial, of Catherine Smyth-Pigott, the 'lawful' widow. She was aged eighty five, and had been in failing health for a considerable time. Throughout she had been devoted to Ruth, and was much liked by all the residents and the villagers who counted it a privilege to know her.

However, the long and so often sensationalised life of the Abode of Love, which might better have borne the title the Abode of Free Love, with its ritual and closely-guarded secrets entered its final stages when Sister Ruth died.

There was now no need for esotery. The real life drama of supposed celestial happiness on the earthly plane reached a climax the week after Easter in 1956. The seclusion was relaxed at last. Not only were villagers and friends in the neighbourhood admitted to the wonderful chapel but representatives of the press for the funeral service—the press which over the years had ruthlessly pilloried the ᶜnonites, taking full advantage of their rigid refusal to grant interviews, and in consequence publishing columns of hocus-pocus and hyperbole.

For the first time and at very short notice we were able to see and

to take photographs of the 'place of worship'. The strident notes of the magnificent organ, one of the finest in the country, greeted us on entering. The pungent aroma of incense filled our nostrils.

Shrouded in black against the east wall stood the altar, furnished with a cross and two highly polished brass candlesticks. The tall white candles were lighted as mourners arrived.

The coffin, resting on trestles draped with golden coloured fabric, was adorned with a mass of spring flowers with trumpet daffodils predominating. The open grave lay before the altar. The sanctuary was reached by a flight of four steps running the width of the chapel. Above the altar hung two large pastoral scenes in oil, painted by members of the community. On one side was the Madonna and Child; on the other a large framed photograph of the 'Ark of the Covenant' church.

Sister Ruth's two sons and daughter were the chief mourners. Agapemonites aged from upwards of seventy to ninety four, with a few retainers, sat on the right. A number of parishioners, and we 'scribes' sat on a higher level at the rear.

A colleague looked around, turned and whispered guilefully, 'We weren't so very far out in our description!'

It was a solemn and intensely impressive service. Yet it served as a reminder of the heresy and hypocrisy that had been enacted within its walls from the aspidistra age of Victoriana until, at least, the late 1920s.

After the opening sentences, the Archbishop of Karin, of the Catholic Apostolic Church of the Good Shepherd, Chelsea, the Most Reverend H. P. Nicholson, D.D., announced that, at the request of the late Mrs Smyth and the community, he had the previous evening consecrated the chapel and its grounds.

Wearing cassock, surplice, and a purple skull cap, he kissed the sons and daughter. His chaplain, the Reverend Paul Craft, in cassock and surplice, swung the thurible while the Archbishop sprinkled holy water over the coffin.

In the spring of 1962 the impenetrable curtain on the whole place finally fell. The property was sold. So numerous were the sightseers that the lane was completely blocked. Cars and the Saturday afternoon bus to town were held up.

◄ **Chapel window at Spaxton.**

Later in the year the organ was dismantled by a well-known Taunton firm of organ builders and removed to the Roman Catholic Church of the Holy Cross at Bedminster, Bristol.

What was to become of the chapel, the reputed centre of a disorderly house; a den of corruption yet a dignified structure of architectural merit and historic interest?

The family, who had survived Pigott, happily and generously refused to allow it to be bulldozed in the name of 'progress' and so suffer the fate of many buildings of note.

The local authority, Bridgwater Rural District Council, gave planning permission for its conversion into a puppet studio. Conditions were that a dangerous tree should be removed, and a lay-by made.

The purchasers were genial Bob Bura, an ENSA entertainer in the war, and his partner, young, tall John Hardwick—both London born but lovers of rural England.

Together this highly talented couple transformed the chapel to meet the requirements of their unusual and very technical profession, stop motion animation. Some while after the funeral of Sister Ruth, I visited the former chapel to have a chat with Bob and John, who make BBC films for education and light entertainment.

It was pleasing to find that the lovely parquet floor and striking lancet windows had been retained. Gone of course, were the altar, the pastoral scenes, and the organ.

At irregular intervals, over a period covering six reigns, the Boer War and two world wars, a peaceful rural parish had suffered the dubious distinction of having the spotlight of the nation on it. The story had been seized on by the sensational sections of the press as first-class copy to be devoured by the masses.

One redeeming feature was that the major events took place before the age of television. Otherwise, the courteous hard-working Spaxtonians would have been subjected to the ignominy of being forced to appear on the screens in millions of homes.

The outbreak of the second world war meant that the Agapemonites were of little interest to Fleet Street, and not much publicity was given, in 1942, to the death of Hamilton, who had been secretary to both Prince and Pigott.

The parallel in the lives of these two renegade eccentrics was that both were ordained in the Church of England, unfrocked for immoral conduct, lived in luxury in a secluded harem, and claimed to be the Redeemer and Saviour of mankind.

Three Graves for a Child on Exmoor

JACK HURLEY

Jack Hurley lived at Williton where he died early in 1984. He was a former editor of The West Somerset Free Press *and contributed to its long running feature 'Notes by the Way'. He loved music and for many years was the organist at Williton Methodist Church. Jack Hurley's published works included* Snow and Storm on Exmoor *and* Murder and Mystery on Exmoor.

The moor was beginning to fold darkly in the late afternoon. It was November.

Into a small grave cut in a hillside churchyard a young clergyman was laying the mangled remains of a murdered girl. It was the third grave for seven-year-old Anna Burgess, but this time she would rest undisturbed.

Two previous graves! The clergyman had sought and found them. He had also directed the hue and cry for a barbarous killer.

William Burgess, slayer of his own daughter, well knew who was his Nemesis. William Thornton, clerk in Holy Orders, first priest of the newly-created ecclesiastical parish of Exmoor, had marked the man as a thoroughgoing rogue months before, accusing him to his face of being a callous killer.

The pair would have a final confrontation, no longer as the hunter and the hunted. In the condemned cell of the county gaol Thornton and Burgess would meet, for the last time, as priest and parishioner. And shake hands.

Thornton was murmuring the last sentences over the little grave. The fading light was merging the land into shapeless grey as he turned away. Across the valley the derelict buildings of the Wheal

Eliza mine became one with the gloom.

This night no mysterious blue light would hover above the mineshaft. There was no longer cause for it. That was what the superstitious folk would be saying.

It had been murder as crude and chilling as the terrain and times against which it was set. Wild the moor, and wild some of its men. This was Exmoor of the 1850s. Its tales of lawlessness, founded on the outlawed Doones, were word of mouth, as yet unwritten, but sixteen years later R.D. Blackmore would turn them into his world-famous *Lorna Doone* romance. The eighteenth-century Doones may have been part fiction, but the desolate moorland was still lending itself to lawlessness and rough living when the Reverend William Thornton came there in 1856 and took up residence in the tiny 'capital' of Simonsbath.

Thornton's arrival was the continuation of a new chapter in the story of ancient Exmoor, a chapter that began in 1818 when John Knight, a Worcestershire businessman who has been called the Cecil Rhodes of the West, bought a large part of the Royal Forest from the Crown and the Acland Estate and embarked on a famous moorland reclamation programme which his son Frederick continued.

The Knights revolutionized the Exmoor scene, though not all their enterprises succeeded. Their main concerns were farming and mining, and the labour entailed meant that the Exmoor clans were infiltrated by outsiders who made the moorland cosmopolitan. There came Scottish shepherds to tend the newly-introduced Cheviot sheep, herdsmen for the black Scottish cattle, Welshmen and Cornishmen for the iron mining, Irish labourers for wall and road building. It was on mining that the Knight hopes mainly rested . . . and ultimately vanished. Iron there was in plenty, but the cost of its transport from such isolated territory was prohibitive, and by the time the Reverend William Thornton came to Exmoor numerous shafts were derelict. Among them, immediately below Simonsbath, where the River Barle flows on its way to join its Exmoor sister, the Exe, was the Wheal Eliza. It was to figure

'To this parish of 22,000 acres came William Thornton as its first priest.' ▶

gruesomely in the Anna Burgess murder story.

When John Knight bought his great acreage of Exmoor it had been stipulated that he should assign land for church purposes at Simonsbath in anticipation of the day when the moorland could show a population of five hundred souls. That day came in 1856; the ecclesiastical parish of Exmoor was created, and the church of St Luke, with a parsonage, built at Simonsbath.

To this parish of 22,000 acres came William Thornton as its first priest. The Knights had done their best to reclaim the land. Could the Church reclaim the people? If that was merely a matter of the health and vigour of a parson, the authorities had made a sound choice. Thornton, however, was under no illusions about his task on this new, cosmopolitan Exmoor of rough ex-miners, unlettered farm labourers, and broken down, non-native farmers who had been attracted to the territory by low rents. Supplementing them were the true natives, but when it came to wild habits of sheer lawlessness, Thornton knew he could make no distinction between the locals and the imported.

Wheal Eliza mine: 'It was to figure gruesomely in the Anna Burgess murder story.'

Thornton was not a Westcountryman by birth, but he had known, and been fascinated by, the Exmoor and North Devon landscape and the character of the people from his youth. Immediately prior to becoming the first priest of the new Exmoor at £150 a year he had been in charge of Countisbury, on the Somerset-Devon coast border, and had helped as curate in Lynton. All for £20 a year.

A young man of twenty-seven, he now settled into Simonsbath, watched his church being built and, on horseback or on foot, re-familiarized himself with the wild terrain he had known as a youth. A man of great physical vigour, he was deliberately defiant of the challenge of the moorland and its weather. A day's thirty-mile walk or a sixty-mile ride on a horse were nothing to him; he even wrote of his 'pleasure' in striking across country on a dark night, knowing that a small error might impound him in a mire. It was nothing to him that his most distant parishioner was twenty-five miles from Simonsbath, or that most of his people were hidden away in cottages in the combes. He sought them out . . . the poor, ill-clad women, the male frequenters of the taverns, the wife and child beaters, the sheep stealers, the rogues of a dozen crude accomplishments.

And in due course the young parson came across William Burgess and his family. They lived in a cottage in a narrow combe near Simonsbath, by the side of the White Water stream, not far from the old Wheal Eliza mine. There was Burgess and his wife and their three children, Tom, Emma and Anna Maria. Burgess was a labourer.

Craftiness corrupting old custom was responsible for the first contact between Burgess and Parson Thornton, and at that moment Thornton mentally registered the man as a rogue to be watched.

Burgess came to the parsonage with a common enough tale of woe. He claimed to have suffered misfortune through losing a pig and a pony and having so much sickness in his family. Would the kind parson help him by drawing up a 'brief' or begging letter so that he could solicit donations towards buying another pig and pony. The 'brief' was an age-old custom in the countryside for touching the sympathies of villagers, and a genuine case rarely failed to evoke a neighbourly response. But the system was open to abuse, and this was a case in point. Thornton fell for the man's tale, prepared a soliciting letter and handsomely headed the subscription list with a guinea . . . only to learn later that he had been conned.

Burgess's pig and pony had died five years ago, and the sickness in the family was an even older episode! Thornton would have felt no more than rueful, and been willing to write off the affair to experience, had it not involved him in an unpleasant scene with an influential parishioner, who accused him of aiding and abetting a rogue to obtain money by false pretences. This rankled with Thornton. Burgess, he decided, was a bad lot. For one thing, his name had been linked with sheep stealing. That, soon, was to play a macabre part in the search for a child's body.

Burgess took his begging letter around the parish and even farther afield, making a highly successful touch. The cash bought him a riotous round of drinking in the South Molton taverns. The bout lasted a whole week.

Thornton was furious. Burgess knew it, and went to every length to keep out of the parson's way. Already, Burgess seemed to be regarding Thornton as a Nemesis. Thornton, riding the lonely tracks, often saw Burgess, but noted that he would turn aside or leap a fence to avoid a meeting. This suited Thornton. If he was putting some measure of fear into the rogue, well and good. But early in 1858 they were in contact again. Burgess's wife died suddenly, and Thornton rode down to the cottage to see if there was anything he could do. Burgess told him that the home would have to be broken up and that he would try to place the three children into service with local households. After several abortive attempts, which he could take as a measure of his unpopularity, Burgess was successful. Tom and Emma were accepted by a family at North Molton. Alas for little Anna; her father took her with him when he obtained lodgings for himself on the outskirts of Simonsbath with a family named Marley. They kept a place known as Gallon House Cot, after the adjoining Gallon House Inn, a name derived from the fact that beer was sold there by the gallon.

Burgess had to find 2s. 6d. a week for the child's maintenance. 2s. 6d., he told himself, that could be better spent in the taverns. Those weekly sums, always paid to Mrs Marley under protest, began to add up to murder.

Summer came to the moorland. It was a Tuesday evening in June when Parson Thornton, riding into Simonsbath, found the parish clerk, Vellacott, and the local forester, Court, talking excitedly.

Thornton reined his horse and smiled down at them. 'What are

30

you two yarning about?' he asked.

'Sir,' said Vellacott in his broad Exmoor, 'little Anna Burgess. Her've disappeared. They can't find her nowheres. They'm all a-saying her father 'av done 'er in.'

Thornton's smile vanished in an instant, but he put aside his private thoughts to lecture the two men on the gravity of making such an allegation. Yet within a few days Thornton would be calling William Burgess 'murderer' to his face.

News had spread slowly. Vellacott and Court told Thornton that Anna had been missing for ten days. The previous Sunday week, at six in the morning, Burgess had left Gallon House Cot with the girl after telling the Marleys he was taking her down to Porlock to lodge her with her grandmother. He was carrying the child's spare clothes in a bundle. That same afternoon he returned without Anna. He stayed at Gallon House Cot until the following Thursday, then left, saying that he, too, had decided to remove to Porlock. He had not been seen since.

The suspicions voiced to Thornton by Vellacott and Court had arisen from the ashes of a fire discovered at the back of the lodgings. Someone had been burning clothes. Mrs Marley, called to take a look, picked up a piece of scorched calico. 'Belongs to Anna's spare frock,' she said.

Thornton passed a troubled night after his encounter with Vellacott and Court. By morning he had decided on action. He sent for forester Court and addressed him with all the authority a parson of those days commanded in his parish.

'Court,' he said, 'you've been party to the spread of rumour. I'm giving you the chance of testing it. Get on my horse and ride down to Porlock. Look in on old Mrs Burgess, but make it appear casual. Say nothing to her about Anna. Just keep your eyes open for her.'

Court returned late in the evening. He had been discreet, and his news was exactly what Thornton had been expecting. Anna Burgess was certainly not in Porlock.

She's in her grave, was Thornton's private thought. Again he acted swiftly. It was late, but he went down to the house of the parish constable, Fry.

'First thing in the morning,' said Thornton, again with a head man's authority, 'ride down to Lynmouth and make inquiries for William Burgess.'

Thornton was playing hunches but every one was to work out for him. If Burgess had a fearful reason for quitting the district—and Thornton was now sure he had—there was no more convenient place to make for than Lynmouth, where some unsuspecting fisherman could ferry him over to Wales.

Leaving Fry, Thornton sought out forester Court again. 'When daylight comes I want you to organize a search for Anna Burgess,' Thornton said. 'Get all the men you can.'

Then . . . 'It's not the child you'll be looking for. It's her grave.'

But for Thornton, daybreak was too long to wait. At 3 a.m. he saddled his horse. He was going to ride forty miles to Curry Rivel, near Taunton, where lived Superintendent Jeffs, the county's chief police officer. Five hours later Thornton was at the superintendent's house. A half hour of earnest conversation, and the parson was on his way back to Exmoor, the superintendent riding at his side.

By noon they were approaching Simonsbath. On the outskirts, by Gallon House, a group of people hailed them. 'We've found the grave,' they shouted.

'And . . .?' rapped Thornton. A man shook his head. 'The grave's empty,' he said.

Thornton and Jeffs rode immediately to the spot. Along ridges of yellow earth, thrown up by mineral prospectors looking for veins, and known as 'deads', the search party had come upon signs of disturbance. Moving the earth, they found in the turf beneath, a small, neatly cut grave with the sods carefully laid on top. They dug into it, but found nothing.

Thornton and the superintendent turned away. In Simonsbath news awaited them. Another of Thornton's hunches had proved correct. Constable Fry was back from Lynmouth, where his inquiries revealed that William Burgess had gone across the Channel to Swansea. A fishing boat had taken him.

Suspicion now carried the strong stench of murder. Jeffs and Fry went down to Lynmouth in the constable's pony-trap. 'We'll cross to Swansea,' said Jeffs.

Meanwhile, Thornton gave orders for a continuing search for the body of Anna. He was convinced that she was no longer alive. Gangs of men poked, peeped and inquired around Simonsbath, but with no result. Thornton, who had been up since 3 a.m. that day, went to bed, but rose early next morning to join the searchers. They spent another fruitless day.

Tired out, Thornton went early to bed. Around midnight he was rudely awakened by stones rattling against his bedroom window. Below stood a group of men.

'What now?' Thornton shouted.

A voice floated up, 'We've got Burgess.'

Thornton paused only to slip on trousers and dressing-gown. He hurried to the constable's house. Fry and Jeffs were there with Burgess. It seemed to Thornton that half the villagers were outside in their nightshirts and bedgowns.

Jeffs and Fry had moved with extraordinary speed in getting over to Swansea, and had had amazing luck in quickly locating Burgess. Now they brought him to the door as Thornton came up. The parson looked steadily at him.

'Burgess,' he said quietly, 'if ever you were in need of a friend it is now. I'm your clergyman and I'll do what I can, but you must tell me what you've done with Anna.'

Burgess spoke no word. Thornton's restraint snapped. 'Murderer,' he shouted as he glared at Burgess. And to the crowd . . . 'Look at him. His silence convicts him. Here he stands the very worst of murderers!'

Dulverton today. Burgess was kept in custody here while inquiries continued.

Even as he turned away in disgust, Thornton knew he had gone too far. Superintendent Jeffs followed him.

'What you've done,' said Jeffs, angrily, 'is to hamper the case by letting Burgess know we haven't found the body. He'll never speak.'

'We'll find the body yet,' promised Thornton, but his tone lacked conviction.

In Burgess's pocket were found a pair of child's boots. Jeffs took them to Gallon House Cot, where Mrs Marley identified them as the pair Anna was wearing when her father took her away.

Jeffs felt justified in taking Burgess to the magistrates at Dulverton, and they ordered him to be kept in custody while inquiries continued.

Every day the search went on around Simonsbath. Summer passed into autumn. Still nothing. Meanwhile, Burgess was in custody and the magistrates became anxious. They told Jeffs they could not hold the man much longer on suspicion. 'Produce a body or we must set him free,' they said.

And then came the break which ensured that Burgess would never again be free. A man, whose identity was never revealed, because that was the price he asked for giving information, came to see Thornton.

The parson's thoughts had turned frequently to the curiosity of the grave among the yellow 'deads' on the trackway to the Wheal Eliza mine. Had it ever contained the body of Anna Burgess? If so, why had the body been disinterred?

Now, as he sat in his parsonage listening to his visitor, Thornton felt a shiver of excitement.

'If I tull 'ee zummat that might be worth 'earing, will 'ee keep quiet about me?' the man had begun.

'Yes,' responded Thornton.

The man and a companion had noticed what looked like a grave among the 'deads'. They concluded that most likely a slaughtered sheep had been buried there. It was not unknown for sheep stealers hastily to bury the carcase, come back for it when it was dark, and cut it up in a cottage for secret distribution. The two men had decided that a dig would yield a worthwhile prize. They had planned to return at night. Meanwhile, they told a third man, a friend, that they thought they had found a sheep buried, and they invited him to share the spoil.

'Who was the man you told?' asked Thornton.

'William Burgess,' was the reply.

Thornton gasped. His mind raced. Now he knew with certainty what had happened. How Burgess must have cursed his ill-luck and the prevalence of sheep-stealing. How he must have been sweating with terror! He alone knew what lay under the sod along the trackway of the 'deads'. He alone must disinter the body of his child . . . and quickly, before his two cronies got there. And this time he would put the body where it would never be found.

The man with Thornton was speaking again. On that Tuesday night in June, he and his companion had arranged to meet Burgess after dark. All three would go to the 'deads' and dig up the sheep's carcase. But Burgess had not turned up, and the other two had developed cold feet. They had decided to forget the matter. However, said the man talking to Thornton, very late that same night he was alone on the hillside above the Wheal Eliza mine ('Never mind what vor, sir'), between the mine and the strange grave, and he had heard footsteps. Someone passed below him, going in the direction of the Wheal Eliza.

The mine! That was it. Thornton was sure the shaft guarded a grisly secret.

There was still nothing positive to go on, but Thornton had grown to trust his hunches. He rode to Dulverton, told the magistrates of his suspicions and obtained a reaction he had hardly dared hoped for. The magistrates said they would order the mine to be emptied of water and searched, and if nothing came of it they would pay the bill themselves. Meanwhile they would continue holding Burgess in custody.

A contractor's tender of £350 for pumping the shaft was accepted. The work was nearly finished in October, but then the machinery broke down and water refilled the mine. It was November by the time the shaft was clear and a descent could be made. 'Send for Parson Thornton,' someone said, inevitably.

Thornton arrived at the mine feeling that he was in some sort of command. He called for a volunteer and a young man stepped forward. Around him they tied a strong rope and he began to descend an old and rotten ladder. Twenty men held the rope to sustain the weight if the ladder gave way. It held, and presently it was apparent that the young man was on the mine floor.

He was not there long. The men above felt a tug on the rope and they began to aid the ascent. No word was spoken. Thornton was

35

conscious of the sounds of exertion and that he himself seemed not to be breathing. Was this, after twenty weeks, to be the moment of truth?

At the surface of the shaft the face of the young man appeared, ghastly in hue from the foul air of the shaft . . . and from something else. In his arms he carried a large parcel tied with cord.

Inevitably, it was Thornton to whom the parcel was handed; Thornton who took a knife and cut the cord, allowing an old tarpaulin jacket to fall away. Underneath was a bag. Thornton slit it, revealing another bag. Again Thornton cut . . . and there was Anna Burgess. A little shift covered her remains. Her face had gone.

The body was carried into a disused and crumbling cottage beside the Wheal Eliza. There was one sound room, secured by lock and key. Thornton put the body inside and pocketed the key. Then he sent a man galloping to Dulverton with the news.

The November afternoon was still bright and fair when three doctors, policemen, a magistrate and a coroner, rode up to the cottage by the Wheal Eliza. Mrs Marley was brought from Gallon House Cot. She said she was able to identify the corpse by the hair and shift. There was no doubt. The pitiful remains had been Anna Burgess.

The coroner asked Thornton to stay with the doctors while they made a post-mortem examination. The spectacle sickened the parson. He was familiar with death, but what he was witnessing now was the sheer mangling of an already pitiful corpse. At the finish the remains were handed to Thornton for Christian burial, and as the sun dipped below the Exmoor hills, Anna Burgess found her final resting place in St Luke's churchyard.

At the same moment, five miles away in Exford, twelve good men and true, hastily rounded up, were holding an inquest on Anna. Their verdict was 'wilful murder by William Burgess'. He was removed from Dulverton to gaol in Taunton. He stood trial at Somerset Assize and was found guilty and sentenced to death.

Thornton, who gave evidence at the trial, was not yet free of the unhappy business which had filled his mind for the last six months. He felt he must visit, as clergyman, the man he had hunted. Burgess agreed to receive him, and it was the most painful hour the parson

Exmoor 140 years on. ▶

ever spent. Burgess would not look at him. He stood facing the wall, his arms over his head. He spoke into the wall, confessing his guilt.

'What made you kill your child?' Thornton asked.

'She was costing me 2s. 6d. a week,' said Burgess. 'And whenever I couldn't find the money Mrs Marley pestered me for it. The child was in the way, sir, and in my way and in everybody else's way, and I thought she would be better out of the way.'

Thornton shuddered at the matter-of-fact statement. There was a long silence. Then Burgess looked round for the first time.

'I want to see my other children,' he said. 'I love that Emma almost as much as the one I killed.'

Speechlessly, Thornton turned to leave the cell.

'I'd like to shake hands with you,' Burgess said. 'You hunted me, but you're a real friend.'

They shook hands.

The indefatigable Thornton rode home to Simonsbath, had a meal, and saddled another horse. He was bound for North Molton, where Tom and Emma Burgess were in service. He must tell these children, who knew nothing of events, that their sister had been murdered by their father and that he was going to be hanged.

Thornton saw Tom alone and began by telling him that his sister Anna was dead.

'Did Father kill her?' asked the twelve-year-old boy. Thornton nodded.

'I always thought Father would do it,' said Tom, calmly.

Both children said they had no wish to see their father, but Thornton prevailed upon them to go, and personally made the travelling arrangements. Burgess wept when the prison governor brought the children to him.

The Burgess affair produced a strange sequel for Thornton. He took action which may have prevented a second child murder on the moor. There had been talk of a repetition. A right scoundrel of a father, lodging in Simonsbath, had with him a little daughter whom he was cruelly ill-using. One day Thornton was told that the man was about to leave Simonsbath and take the child with him. The prospect of a dead parallel with the Burgess tragedy did not strike Thornton as forcibly as it did his wife. Mrs Thornton became agitated, cried that the child was going to be murdered, and demanded that Thornton should intervene before it was too late.

It was nightfall and rain was teeming, but so insistent was Mrs Thornton that the parson went at once to the lodging house to see the child's father. What followed must have been one of the strangest business transactions ever conducted. Thornton was, in effect, buying a six-year-old girl off her father. The terms, agreed and witnessed to by the keeper of the lodging house, were that the father should pay Thornton 2s. 6d. a week, and he (Thornton) would clothe, board, educate and generally provide for the girl until she could be put out into the world in a respectable position.

Thornton came back to the parsonage dripping wet. The deal had been conducted with the parson standing outside the lodging house, talking up to the father, who had his head out of the bedroom window.

But Mrs Thornton was happy.

On the morning of 4 January 1859, the black flag was hoisted above Taunton Gaol. From a platform in full view of the public, hangman Calcraft gave William Burgess the death-drop.

In Simonsbath the superstitious were saying it should have been realized from the first that Anna's body was down the mine. Had not a strange blue light hovered above the shaft each night? Now it was seen no more.

There was a widespread belief that William Burgess died with more on his conscience than the killing of his child . . . that he was a fire-raiser who caused the deaths of three people. It was an incident that had a direct bearing on the subsequent fate of little Anna.

After the death of his wife Burgess tried first to place Anna with a family in the Exmoor parish of Withypool. He went to a house known as South Hill and asked James Hayes and his wife Sarah if they would accept Anna. It was not convenient, because Sarah already had a child and was bearing another.

Burgess became fiendishly angry. On the night of 13 January 1858, he took mad revenge on the South Hill family, setting fire to the house. James Hayes and his wife escaped from the blaze, but James's father, John Hayes, aged sixty three, and two others who were staying in the house, Matthew Shapland (twenty two) and Grace Shapland (twelve) died from suffocation and burns. They are buried in Withypool churchyard. Had Anna Burgess been taken into this home she would have been safe, and three more people would have been spared a horrifying death.

William Burgess came out of the gallows platform with one fear
. . . that among the people come to watch him die he would see the
faces of Exmoor friends.

Friends? Was it possible?

(*Author's note:* Mr Robert C. Hayes, of High Wycombe, a great-
great-grandson of John Hayes, of South Hill house, has written to
me about the fire in which his forebear and two others perished. It
was always understood in the family, says Mr Hayes, that William
Burgess confessed to the arson while he lay under sentence of
death.)

Woods on the Blackdown Hills.

Some Somerset Curiosities

HILARY WREFORD

Hilary Wreford is a Devonian, a Capricorn subject born at Brixham. She trained as a nurse and now operates as a part-time Community Nurse in and around Okehampton. Has contributed features on Dartmoor subjects to both The Okehampton Times *and* The Tavistock Times *and, in the last two years, has done research for three Bossiney titles. This is her debut as a Bossiney author.*

Somerset is more than a county of contrasts. It has a landscape and a history containing more than its share of curiosities.

According to the *Collins English Dictionary*, a curiosity is 'something strange or fascinating', and this county of cider and cricket—and cheese—underlines that description. Admittedly time, fashion and fad *and* neglect all help to establish what is a curiosity —and what is not.

Take, for example, this lovely Somerset landscape, so wealthy in man-made follies. Barwick Park boasts as many as four such oddities, all the brain children in the early nineteenth century of George Messiter. When a slump came in the glove-making industry, Mr Messiter, with commendable vision, offered work to several of the unemployed—building these statements in stone—and eccentricity.

They stand, like sentries, on each boundary line of Barwick Park. There is Jack the Treacle Eater, reputed to represent a young man, a member of Messiter's work force who made trips to London and back *on foot*—and kept his strength up by consuming huge quantities of treacle. He—Jack the Treacle Eater—slightly resembles Eros and even today dominates the eastern skyline.

41

Then there is the round Fish Tower. Nowadays you would rightly ask 'Why Fish Tower?' because it stands derelict among the trees. Time was when it was surmounted by a fish-shaped weather vane.

Folly number three is a leaning obelisk on the southern edge. It looks as if it might topple any day—or hour.

Arguably the most elegant of this strange quartet is Messiter's Cone marking the western boundary. Four arches support a tapered cone, punctured by square holes. The cone rises to some seventy feet—four feet longer than a wicket on the county ground at Taunton—its smooth top portion set off by a sphere.

If the ghost of George Messiter haunts this corner of Somerset, he doubtless chuckles when finding his follies still peopling this parkland. Long may they stand.

And what of the ghost of the Earl of Chatham, Prime Minister and father of William Pitt, our youngest Prime Minister? Does he haunt Curry Rivel?

When Sir William Pynsent died, he left Burton House and his estate to the Earl, a politician whom he greatly admired, and Pitt, the Elder, in due course erected his column at Curry Rivel.

Originally it provided magnificent views over Sedgemoor, that historic and some say haunted battlefield. But today's visitor is denied that bird's eye view—and all because of one cow. This animal, belonging to a Curry Rivel farmer, incredibly squeezed her way to the top, and fell to her death. To prevent any further disasters, the entrance was sealed.

The Wellington Obelisk built on the Blackdown Hills is another Somerset landmark, serving as a permanent and deserved memorial to the Iron Duke and his great victory at Waterloo. As a bonus it has often been said the finest views can be obtained of Exmoor and Brendon from the monument; and no doubt many of the climbers who have made the arduous ascent up the 235 narrow steps, and, finding it well worth while, have reflected that the monument had been erected for 'Wellington's favourite son'.

Well, I am afraid that nothing is farther from the truth, as the Duke of Wellington had, at the time the monument was built, never visited the Town! In fact the only reason he chose Wellington as the

The Wellington Obelisk, built on the Blackdown Hills, is another Somerset landmark. ▶

Wellington Monument.

44

title for his peerage was that he liked the name, and the Wellesley family did have some minor connection with the town.

Certainly the nation was grateful for the Iron Duke's success at Waterloo; and Wellington Town itself was happy that its name was to be used in this way—so much so that a committee of local worthies was formed, with the idea of perpetuating his memory.

A Westcountry man, Thomas Lee of Barnstaple, was commissioned to draw up a suitable scheme. Expecting a large sum to be donated, an extravagant expensive scheme was produced, not only to provide the monument, but also three cottages were to be built with the splendid idea of providing accommodation for three wartime veterans. In addition a number of brass cannons were to be obtained as a result of Waterloo and displayed; large circular steps were to be constructed at the base of the monument, and the whole project completed by capping it with a large statue of the Duke to be made, I believe, in cast iron. The money was not as forthcoming, and the scheme had to be curtailed with the result that for many years it remained unfinished. Indeed, it was not until 1854 that the well-known triangular top was added.

Well, if the town and district seemed grateful and for a relatively small community raised a large sum of money, the Duke of Wellington did very little to familiarise himself with the area.

It seems that although some reputed 10,000 people attended the Foundation Stone laying ceremony, the Duke was not able to be present, and it was not until two years later in 1819 that he made his one and only visit to this part of Somerset. I often wonder if the imposing statue of himself had been there to crown his monument, would he have found the time to admire it—and make further visits before he died in 1852?

Stone circles have long fascinated me. Certainly the legends surrounding many of them encourage us to believe that the very Devil himself has strong connections.

The three stone circles near to the village of Stanton Drew are typical. These stones, to this day, are known as the 'Devil's Wedding' or just 'The Wedding'.

It all began many years ago, when like so many of us, a local

◀ Duke of Wellington.

couple chose Saturday as their wedding day. Following the ceremony there was to be much merry making and the happy couple had selected fields adjacent to the village for their 'reception'. We, of course, will never know what actually happened, as the River Drew which still wanders along so peacefully was perhaps the only witness to the proceedings.

It all started well, the music being provided by a piper, with the bride happily entering the festivities, but at the bewitching hour of midnight the mood of the party changed. It is often said that 'the piper calls the tune', and this was no exception, for suddenly the piper announced that as it was now the Sabbath he would no longer play—and packed away his instrument.

Whereas the bride had been so happy, the mood dramatically changed. She lost her temper, but the piper still adhered to his principles and refused to play on the Sabbath. There are several versions as to what followed, but the one I tend to believe is where the bride became so angry that she demanded that another piper be produced so that the party could continue—and is quoted to have said that if necessary she would go to Hell to obtain one! Whether she had to go to this extreme or not, I do not know, but suddenly out of the darkness appeared an old man who not only seemed to be a musician, but had the good fortune to have his musical instrument with him. Our bride seems to have been difficult to please as, far from expressing gratitude for the new piper at stepping into the breach, she complained bitterly at the sedate way he was playing. The piper seems to have made every effort to please as he accelerated, getting faster and faster with all the guests joining in. The mood and speed of the music whipped them into a frenzy—and although they needed a rest the piper went on and on playing throughout the night. Indeed it is now apparent that the piper was the Devil himself and only returned to Hell when he was satisfied that no-one survived and he had reduced the party to a group of grinning skeletons.

In the quiet of the morning and, perhaps with the dew still on the ground, curious villagers visited the fields and found to their horror that the wedding party or the skeletons no longer existed—instead

'I wonder what happened to the faithful cow . . .
if her spirit still wanders around Somerset . . .' ▶

just the stones we know today appropriately as the 'Devil's Wedding'.

If I said there was no witness just the river, I was possibly in error as legend says that just one man remained: the village piper, who had witnessed the entire scene and who was found hiding under the hedge, albeit half dead with fright.

Who could blame him for his incoherent description of what had happened that fateful night?

Many strange happenings have taken place at Watchet, but the story of St Decuman is one of horror and yet at the same time one of spiritual awakening. St Decuman was not a Westcountryman—he came from Wales—not making the journey by land but instead choosing the hazardous journey across the Severn. Moreover if legend is to believed, he made it on his 'cloak'. Personally I feel that a more substantial craft was used, a simple coracle perhaps.

There is no doubt that the reason he chose Watchet was that he was seeking a place where he could live simply in peace and tranquillity. After his successful landing he made his way up the nearest hill and proceeded to construct a shelter from where he could base his activities. Here he continued to live and eke out a simple living, with his only companion, a faithful cow, whose milk provided him with the basis of his simple diet.

St Decuman was an extremely religious man, and after the completion of his shelter built a small place where he could worship in solitude and this is said to be the site of the present church.

His idyllic existence continued for many years, and no doubt would have continued for many more, but one fateful day he 'chanced' upon a Danish invader, who had no respect for St Decuman's peaceful life. It is said that the Dane simply and without further thought swiftly beheaded our unfortunate worthy. Here the story might have ended—and never have been recorded—but to the horror of the Dane, St Decuman stopped, picked up his head, washed it clean of all the blood then proceeded to lay it by his side before departing this mortal life. Whilst no doubt this would have been horrific for anyone it certainly made a lasting impression on our Danish invader as it is said he was immediately 'converted', becoming a man of religion.

The corpse rose from the coffin shouting for help. ▶

Whilst this tells the story of the demise of this poor unfortunate man, I have always wondered what happened to the faithful cow, whether she was a witness to that dreadful killing and if her spirit still wanders around the Somerset countryside looking for her friend and master.

The church itself stands above the town, and has many interesting features a large number of them relating to the well-known Wyndham family who were so proud of their place of worship, and played such a part in its history. It is about one member of this family, one Florence Wyndham, that I must unfurl one particularly grim story; a story without equal I think and one which I must emphasise has always been accepted *as fact*.

Not long after her marriage Florence was taken ill, lapsed into a coma and to all intents and purposes died. In the parlance of the medical profession of today she was pronounced 'clinically dead'. All the necessary arrangements were made for her funeral and she was laid to rest in her coffin in the church with candles burning at each end. There was much grief and sadness within the family and the district at the passing of the young bride, not least from her sorrowing husband. Here the story might have finished but for the

Watchet Church stands above the town.

Harold Gimblett, a man who truly
became a legend in his cricketing lifetime.

avarice of the sexton who had been left in the church to watch over the body. I suppose that as he was alone in the church with the body he could not dismiss from his mind the thought of the beautiful rings which she wore—and whether they would be buried with her. One can imagine him in the silent church lifting the coffin lid very slowly, and sure enough in the candlelight he could see the rings sparkling. It was at this moment that his greed overcame any principles, and one can visualise him with his heart pounding, leaning over the still coffin and proceeding to remove the rings.

He was however to receive the shock of his life: the so-called 'corpse' rose from the coffin and shouted for help! White with fright, he ran screaming from the church and, as a result, the family was alerted—and hurried to the church in disbelief. It was a happy end as Mrs Wyndham was able to return home apparently none the worse for her 'premature death' and was happily able to bear a son—and outlive her husband by many years.

I have often wondered what happened to the sexton; whether he was punished for his attempted 'crime' or whether the family were grateful that his greed had saved the life of the young Florence.

My husband Michael, a keen cricketer, says I have left out the best Watchet legend: Harold Gimblett, a man who truly became a legend in his cricketing lifetime. Playing for Somerset from 1935 until 1954—the war years excepted—he scored 49 centuries for his county, twice passed 2,000 runs in a season, and scored more than 1,000 runs in a dozen seasons. Gimblett amassed 23,000 runs in first-class cricket, yet played only three times for England—he was chosen to tour India in the winter of 1939-40 but Hitler had other ideas.

He gave immense pleasure to cricket lovers all over Somerset and far beyond the old county boundaries. Sadly he took his own life in March 1978. It is a remarkable story, and has been told brilliantly by David Foot in his book *Harold Gimblett, Tormented Genius of Cricket.*

Midnight Poachers at East Coker

DAVID FOOT

David Foot writes regularly on cricket, soccer and Rugby for various newspapers, including The Guardian *and* The Sunday Express. *He has worked in radio and television and is the author of several books. His* Harold Gimblett, Tormented Genius of Cricket, *is rated one of the finest cricket books of its kind. 'There has never been a cricket book quite like this,' wrote John Arlott. 'David Foot has written it with compassion, something not too far from passion, and sympathy. It is a remarkable achievement . . .'*

Nathaniel Cox was a village policeman. He was well-built, good-looking, brave and, as perhaps he needed to be in that exacting job of his a century ago, mildly arrogant. He was on nodding, occasionally cider-drinking terms with most of his fellow parishioners at East Coker. He was a devoted husband and father of four young children.

And on the pitch-black night of 16 November 1876 just before midnight he was kicked and bludgeoned to death.

It was a crime that outraged the whole of the Westcountry. Austere local newspapers, loth to change the size of their headline whether they were reporting a bun-fight or a Royal jubilee, suddenly took on a campaigning fervour. They increased the size of their type as they chronicled the ensuing progress over *The Yeovil Policeman Murder.*

Some of the national papers, too, caught the mood of Somerset anger. They, too, graphically recounted the details of PC Cox's injuries. Paradoxically, readers were hardly squeamish in those days.

This is what had happened in a narrow, tortuous country lane, between Netherton and Sutton Bingham and less than a mile from Coker Marsh, East Coker, that damp and gusty November night.

53

It was the eve of Yeovil Fair. That often meant trouble for the police—and they knew it. Yeovil would become crowded with strangers, some of them swigging more ale than was wise. The cheapjacks would arrive; and so, less lawfully, would the pick-pockets. The farmers would converge on the town—and so would the horse thieves and poachers.

Senior police officers, although hardly in the Softly-Softly class, held their briefings. Poachers, it seemed, became their priority. The directive had gone out: 'There's too much poaching. Intensify the patrols.' Maybe the impassioned order was influenced by the number of country squires who were apt to sit on the local Benches —between game shoots, that was!

Nathaniel Cox received his instructions and privately looked forward to the challenge. He was thirty-seven, broad in the shoulders and thick in the fists. He could look after himself. His neighbours spoke of him with affection and knew he enjoyed local popularity. There was a touch of bravado, at times, when he assured friends it would be a rash gipsy or poacher who took *him* on.

The police obviously intended taking no chances that particular night. The constables were to patrol in pairs. Cox's mate was to be Henry Stacey, stationed at nearby West Coker. He had been in the Force for three years and had neither Cox's experience nor physical stature.

It's also likely that Stacey was a little more apprehensive. At any rate, he nipped into the White Post Inn and had a drink before going on duty.

At ten o'clock that night, and several drinks later, Cox and Stacey were at Netherton when they heard a horse and cart coming towards them. A gruff, self-conscious exchange of good nights was followed by a significant darting look between the two policemen who were carrying a lantern.

They recognized the three men in the cart and they had a suspicion that there was another lying on his back in the bottom of the cart. They couldn't be sure and there were, after all, no grounds for stopping the men and questioning them.

Just under two hours later, the two policemen were having a glass

PC Cox's headstone at East Coker:
'. . . killed whilst in the discharge of his duty.' ▶

IN MEMORY OF
NATHANIEL COX
A POLICE CONSTABLE OF THIS
COUNTY WHO WAS KILLED WHILST
IN THE DISCHARGE OF HIS DUTY
ON THE NIGHT OF NOVEMBER 16. 1870
AGED 37

IN THE HOUR OF DEATH, AND IN THE DAY
OF JUDGMENT. GOOD LORD. DELIVER US.

of ale in the nearby home of Farmer Squibb when their hunch paid off. They heard the horse and cart making its return journey. Cox and Stacey quietly followed. There was now one man sitting at the front of the cart; three others were walking. It looked as though the cart was now loaded with something.

The cart creaked round the sharp bend where the railway bridge now stands and began the sharp rise up Netherton Lane. The horse slowed and it was obvious to the police officers that there was more than an empty cart behind. Cox, the more assertive of the two policemen, decided it was the moment for action.

He suddenly ran forward and seized the reins.

'What have you got in the cart?'

'It's no business of yours.'

'We intend to search and see.'

'Let go this hoss.'

'You will have to kill me first.'

'We will do for both of the buggers.'

Stacey, all this time at the tail of the cart and trying to look inside, heard a blow struck. He ran towards Cox and found him sprawled on the road, his helmet knocked off.

Cox gasped: 'They've got me. Look out, they're coming again!'

Now the men started beating Stacey about the head. He tried to use his staff but they smothered him with blows. One vicious clout to the side of the head sent him plunging into the ditch. Soon he was unconscious.

Stacey came to, face down, in the ditch. The cart had gone. There was no sound.

He staggered to his feet and felt the wet blood on his head, trickling down his face. He had no idea what had happened to Cox. Gradually he was able to focus his eyes and he saw a dim light in the distance. Stacey climbed through the hedge at the side of the road and set off across the fields in the direction of the light. Several times he half-collapsed.

It was Darvill Farm. The seriously injured policeman hammered on the door. Farmer Henry Marsh pulled some warm clothes over his night-shirt. He found Stacey, leaning against the wall of the house. As coherently as possible, Stacey blurted out the details of the attack.

Farmer Marsh knocked up two of his labourers who lived a few hundred yards away. They quickly hitched-up a waggon and went, with Stacey, back to Netherton Lane.

Seventy or so yards from where the first blows were struck they found Cox. He was dead. His cape and his helmet were discovered some distance away. And his staff was broken, near his limp hand.

Cox's body was lifted on to the waggon and taken, along with Stacey, to the New Inn, East Coker. It was placed in an outhouse and Dr E.C. Garland was sent for. The doctor had known Nathaniel Cox for many years. He had attended him and his family. But he could hardly recognize him as he lay on the rough floor of that pub outhouse.

As Dr Garfield said later in evidence: 'I found that he had a compound comminuted fracture of the scalp on the left side of the head. On that side, the brain was protruding. The left ear was badly lacerated.' He thought the terrible injuries could have been caused by a succession of heavy kicks.

While the doctor made his grisly examination of Cox at the New Inn, Stacey was himself in a bad way. He had severe concussion. He was taken to hospital where he remained for some weeks, initially in a critical condition.

East Coker knew of the tragedy within hours. Early farm and estate workers discovered the macabre ritual at the inn as they set off for work.

'Nat Cox is dead. The poachers got him!'

Rosy-faced village housewives, their cheeks shining from a cursory wash in cold water, ghoulishly gossiped in little knots around the pub's back-yard. But they were hustled away.

'Ah, 'tis true. Policeman Cox is done for. There's nothing you can do. Off you go.'

'But what about his kiddies? He's got four of them. Who'll look after them and his missus?'

Such questions remained unanswered.

The Westcountry papers soon picked up the story. One, renowned for its caution and contempt for the slightest sniff of sensationalism, stormed into print. It mentioned the Hutchings family as well-known local poachers. One of the sons, it informed its readers, had recently been in prison for assault on the police. Would any news editor dare to print such an innuendo nowadays?

One report said of the dead policeman: 'He was very tall and imposing and one of the smartest in the Division.'

A police notice was also circulated. Here, too, names were being freely given:

MURDER! ABSCONDED FROM HARDINGTON, CHARGED WITH THE MURDER OF P.C. COX ON THE NIGHT OF NOV. 16 AT NETHERTON—GEORGE HUTCHINGS ABOUT 55 YEARS, 5FT 6INS TALL, DARK HAIR TURNING GREY, SALLOW COMPLEXION, THIN FACE. GILES HUTCHINGS ABOUT 30, 5FT 7INS, BLACK HAIR, WHISKERS AND MOUSTACHE, SALLOW COMPLEXION, THIN FACE AND DOWNCAST LOOK. PETER HUTCHINGS ABOUT 26, 5FT 6INS, RATHER STOUT, DARK BROWN HAIR, SALLOW COMPLEXION MARKED WITH SMALLPOX. INFORMATION TO SUPT SMITH, OF YEOVIL.

Netherton Lane: 'Just before midnight, he was kicked and bludgeoned to death.'

The Hutchings family were, indeed, notorious poachers and had had a number of skirmishes with the law. Their shifty looks and abusive manners won them few friends in Hardington, where they lived, or in East and West Coker. Every policeman in Yeovil knew them. They had obviously been recognized by Cox and Stacey. But who was the fourth member on that fateful ride through the night towards and back from the direction of the Dorset border?

The answer was not long coming. Charles Baker, who lived at West Coker, was soon found and taken to Yeovil where he was charged with being concerned in the murder of Cox. The three others made a mysterious disappearance.

The police mounted a search extraordinarily thorough for the 1870s when communicating was a laborious process. Reports filtered through. The three missing poachers were spotted at Charminster, Puddletown and Okeford Fitzpaine. They stopped once for ale at a Shillingstone inn. Once they were seen washing at a brook alongside the road at Beaminster.

A trail of false information, all well-meaning, hindered the hunt. Once a group of policemen, hurriedly mustered, boarded a train on the old Wilts and Somerset line. It was an unavailing hunch.

And as the weeks went by, the public became more uneasy. Rumours increased. Would men, desperate enough to club a policeman to death, be prepared to strike again? There were veiled hints that the murder of PC Cox had a link with the killing of a woman called Ruth Butcher two years before. It was alleged that one of the accused men had been intimate with her.

A spate of attacks, including murders, by poachers on policemen all over Britain about this time heightened the anxiety.

But how long could the three Hutchings last out—without much food? The theory gained weight that they had made their way back, by night, to Hardington or West Coker. Perhaps someone was now harbouring them.

Then there was a surprise development in late January. A butcher from West Coker called James Vagg arrived outside Yeovil police station in his horse and cart. His load: old George Hutchings and his son, Giles. They were dishevelled and haggard.

Vagg claimed he had found them by accident not far from his home village and that they had said they were prepared to give themselves up. As a rather well-rehearsed after-thought, Vagg contended that he qualified for the £100 reward that was being offered.

The police had them in and took statements. It was something they had hardly expected. James Vagg, too, seemed a little too plausible. As one policeman said at the time: 'It's all too bloody cut and dried.'

What had happened to Peter—or young 'George'—Hutchings? The Deputy Chief Constable of Somerset was now firmly in control of the investigations. He ordered a search of the West Coker butcher's premises and eventually the third poacher was found hiding under some timber in a loft. He was too weak to resist.

Now all four were behind bars. They appeared at Yeovil Magistrates' Court on 30 January. And, with one of those quirks of human nature, the hearing was something of a social occasion. There were seven magistrates, all dressed in their Sunday best. The Mayor of Yeovil was given a special seat just below the Bench. The public, thousands of them, thronged around the Town Hall.

The case should have started at 10 a.m. It got under way at 11.30. Charge: murder of PC Cox and attempted murder of PC Stacey.

The prisoners had been brought from Taunton and they were 'ironed' as they came into court. Later, permission was given for the irons to be removed.

Stacey gave his evidence clearly although he was still shaky from his ordeal. He was cross-examined about the drinking done by the two police officers that night.

'I had a little to drink that night—but not much. I went just inside the Red House Inn at Stoford where we both had some ale. I couldn't afford beer (laughter).'

He also admitted that they went into a house for some cider, as well as having something to drink at Farmer Squibb's. Yes, and he (Stacey) did have a quick drink before going on duty.

'The last place we went to before the murder was Farmer Squibb's and when we left we were quite sober.'

Sarah Squibb, the farmer's wife, told the magistrates she drew the pair a small jar of ale. They had come to the house in the first place to ask about some gipsies.

Then into the witness-box went Farmer Henry Marsh. His gnarled outdoor fingers uneasily gripped the woodwork in front of him. His rubicund cheeks twitched nervously. He was happier doing the milking.

He described the bump on Stacey's head, when he staggered to the door, as 'the size of a hen's egg'. And Farmer Marsh said that

Cox had received 'enough blows to kill ten men . . . his brains were coming from his skull'.

The four defendants were committed for trial to Taunton Assize in the March.

Meanwhile, Vagg was charged with concealing and harbouring Peter Hutchings. The number of testimonials handed in on his behalf was impressive. A farmer, businessman, carpenter and even a Yeovil JP were called for the defence. He was discharged and went back to his unpretentious butcher's shop a grateful and maybe lucky man—without the £100 reward money, we imagine.

The trial itself was something out of black comedy, at least at the start. Here, after all, was a drama with most of the elements that whet a bloodthirsty public's appetite. The murder itself was one of the most brutal ever remembered in the Westcountry. The prisoners were well-known local villains in the pre-judgement of the public. The victim was no back-alley drunkard but an officer of the law. And the fact that the accused, all except Baker, had eluded the police for two months provided an added touch of fiction-style action for a public which craved gossip, excitement and outrage to offset their own mundane lives.

Nearly two hours before the Shire Hall opened its doors, the long flight of steps leading to the public gallery was crammed.

The wing-collared scribe on *The Western Daily Press* wrote in tut-tutting horror of the scene: 'A more unseemly spectacle than that presented when admission was granted to the public can scarcely be imagined. The scene on Boxing Night at the theatre may have equalled it—a hurrying and excited crowd racing up the stairs and leaping over the benches and then, amid rough jokes, struggling for the best seats.'

It was bad enough getting the jury seated. When their names were called they had to fight their way to the places allocated to them.

The Lord Chief Justice, Sir Alexander Cockburn, fidgeted with growing impatience. Suddenly he boomed: 'Who is the Chief of the Constabulary force?'

Mr Bisgood: 'I am, sir. But we aren't responsible for order in the court.'

'But you *are* responsible for bringing a sufficient number of officers to preserve order.'

'We would, if we'd received notice. I'll do what I can, My Lord.'

Commotion there may have been in court. But the four prisoners appeared surprisingly calm in the dock. Giles Hutchings was officially described on the court-sheet as a glover, the other three as labourers. In evidence, the Hutchings were also said to be small dealers.

In his opening speech for the prosecution, Mr Collings QC said that when Baker was apprehended he was wearing heavy boots. Some human hairs were found on them but they were not necessarily Cox's.

Superintendent Charles Smith said that the instructions to the two policemen were to patrol the neighbourhood 'as we have done for the last twenty years at Fair time. There were a number of evil-disposed persons congregated in the area.'

Mr W. Molesworth St Aubyn, for the defence, asked the superintendent about taking Baker to the police station.

'Was there some inducement held out to the prisoner to say something? Had there not been a reward put out, offering £100 to anyone not a policeman, who could give information?'

'No, that was at a subsequent time.'

'Had there been a prior reward of £30?'

'No.'

At the end of the first day's hearing, the jury were locked away in a local hotel for the night. Two bailiffs were put in charge of them.

And then came the second day—'with more disgraceful scenes'. In fact, the lawyers had great difficulty entering the courtroom. So had the press. Police were kept busy curbing free fights that broke out in the street. A few well-known Westcountry poachers, dubious small dealers and gipsies were among those trying to get into the courtroom, presumably to give the Hutchings and Baker moral support.

In his closing speech for the prosecution, Mr Collings said: 'These men were acting together and, if the jury find that, it does not matter which of them struck the blow—if there is a common intention either to murder or to do grievous bodily harm and death ensues . . .'

His Lordship, who at this point went out of his way to ensure that the prisoners were given a fair trial—no doubt to balance out the considerable prejudice which was a feature of the case—interrupted:

'Up to the time of stopping the cart, I don't see a tittle of evidence that there was any intention to kill.'

Inevitably, the defence were not going to ignore the police officer's intermittent liquid refreshment on the night of the crime.

'I'm not going to suggest,' said Mr St Aubyn (immediately doing the opposite) 'that they were the worst for liquor during the unfortunate affray—at all events, not tipsy. But, in fact, it was admitted that they had gone to various places and drunk several glasses of ale and cider. When the cart passed by the house of Mr Squibb, the constables had probably had a little more drink than was absolutely necessary for their health.

'The Hutchings and Baker were out that night, as they had a perfect right, with a pony and trap . . . Cox, without the slightest authority or excuse, marched up to the pony's head and stopped it. Could they believe otherwise than that he had his staff drawn? A constable had no right to stop the cart unless he had reasonable grounds for suspecting a felony had been committed.'

Mr St Aubyn was a wily operator. He knew that he had a shaky defence and he knew the considerable emotional climate that had built up against his clients. But there was still psychology. He paused and looked at the jurors one by one.

'If you cannot without a shadow of doubt point a finger at any one of the prisoners and say that he killed Cox, you must acquit the prisoners of the charge of murder.'

It all seemed to depend on His Lordship's wording. 'When Cox met his death, it was by foul means, both gross and brutal. . . . That the violence was the act of some, if not all of the prisoners is, I feel, clear. But as to how and in what precise circumstances the constable met his death we are left absolutely in the dark.'

His Lordship spoke for ninety minutes. He left the jury with a strong feeling of uncertainty about what actually happened. It was an impression hardly shared by the hundreds who waited in the street outside the Shire Hall for the verdict. They were already putting the rope round the head of the four defendants.

The jury were out for forty-five minutes. They came back and announced that they found the three Hutchings and Baker guilty of manslaughter. There was a gasp of disbelief around the Assize.

His Lordship: 'The jury have taken a merciful view of your case and I think have acted wisely, too. I don't think this was a case of premeditated murder . . . But I must pass upon you a sentence of long and weary servitude little better than slavery. If I have any doubt about the case at all, it is whether I have not been too lenient.'

He decided that the older Hutchings had taken no part at all in the attack and gave him a free pardon. The other three were given twenty-four years.

There had been one dramatic interruption immediately before sentence. Baker, in his gruff voice, said: 'Beg pardon, my Lord. I should like to speak up for the old man. Truth is truth and he didn't leave the cart.'

His Lordship: 'I am glad to hear you say that. I will give his case special consideration.'

And so the four Somerset poachers left the dock—one for a tense, finger-pointing freedom, the others for penal servitude. Old Hutchings was already a broken man. His familiar dealer's cart was rarely seen again.

Widow Mrs Cox, befriended by her neighbours in East Coker, struggled to bring up her four young children. And she told, in time, an uncanny story.

On the night before her husband's death he hardly slept at all. When he finally woke from a fitful half-sleep, he turned to her and said:

'I've had a bad time. I dreamt that I had a fight with some gipsies and they gave me a horrible smack just here (he tapped his head).'

A doctor confirmed that when he went to break the news of her husband's death to Mrs Cox, she cut in with the words: 'I know. He's killed, isn't he?'

A tombstone just inside the churchyard at East Coker commemorates the bravery of PC Nathaniel Cox, 'killed in the discharge of his duty'.

We shall never know which of the poachers struck Cox the fatal blow. There was loyalty among villains in the dock at the Shire Hall, Taunton.

Many Westcountrymen—and women—were angered by the verdict.

In fact, Somerset can seldom, if ever, have had a more harrowing crime. As a boy I never walked along the steep, winding Netherton Lane, claustrophobic under the high hedgerows and oddly frightening, without re-living the grim midnight details of a century ago.

East Coker has various claims to fame. Dampier the explorer was born there and Eliot the poet wrote about it. If they both, in their different ways, stir the imagination, so sadly—after a hundred years—does Cox the policeman.

Hauntings

LORNIE LEETE-HODGE

Lornie Leete-Hodge was born and lives in Wiltshire, but has strong links with Somerset through her mother who was born in Weston-super-Mare. An editor by profession, she is a former editor of Wessex Life *and other magazines, and author of a number of books including four on Wiltshire, two novels, children's books, a Royal Wedding book and a best-selling biography of* Diana, Princess of Wales. *When not writing she edits other people's books!*

Somerset, feast of legend and mystery, is steeped in peaceful tranquillity with little streams, gentle villages set against the grandeur and wildness of Exmoor, and brooding hills with their hint of secrets. Each part has its own special aura and atmosphere clinging from its past, sometimes happy, sometimes sad. The county has been described as a 'legend laden land' and where better to seek ghosts and hauntings?

Exmoor with its wonderful scenery, enveloping mists, hidden quagmires reminds the traveller that nature is in control, and the sense of legend is so strong one would not be surprised to meet a Doone or the gallant John Ridd. Time has not intruded too greatly into this area which will preserve its legends, seemingly for ever.

A terrible sadness seems to pervade the Sedgemoor area and places associated with the ill-fated Duke of Monmouth Rebellion when so many brave young Somerset men who followed a fruitless cause were so ruthlessly slaughtered. To this day the tragedy of

◀'Somerset, feast of legend and mystery, is steeped in peaceful tranquillity . . .'

those wasted lives still seems to cry for vengeance, and the stain of blood spilt remains.

By contrast, feelings at Glastonbury are of quiet and love, and it is easily credible that Christ came here leaving His own unique calm. So the romantic Arthurian legend with handsome knights, lovely ladies and brave deeds finds a resting place in the King's grave. The peace of the Tor, the ruins and its secrets which have puzzled minds over the centuries—surely no-one can leave this place without in some way feeling changed.

So much for the main legends and hauntings of this lovely county. By comparison the rest pale, but they need not be forgotten and this chapter is a reminder.

There are many tales surrounding the Arthurian legend, but this one concerns the villages of West and Queen Camel where, to the north, are traces of a causeway. Best seen when the spring grass is growing or from the air, it is the track along which Arthur is said to ride out at the head of his knights on Midsummer's Eve. What a wonderful sight!

Sedgemoor: '. . . the stain of blood
spilt remains.'

A phantom of a much later king, Henry II, is also connected with this area. A visitor in the early 1920s was surprised to see a large house standing in a field which she had not noticed on previous walks. As a stranger, she saw nothing abnormal in the house, though it looked both solid and very old, and she paid little heed. Then she noticed a man and a small boy standing by the door and was struck by their unusual clothes. They seemed to be staring straight at her. She stood still wondering whether to speak to them, and both the house and the figures disappeared. One moment they were facing her—the next they had gone.

She made enquiries, but no trace of a house could be discovered. It was later learned that Prince Henry lived in Somerset as a child, in hiding as a safety precaution during the wars between King Stephen and Matilda, and the exact location was a well-kept secret. So the woman probably saw the ghosts of the young prince and his guardian.

Near Blagdon in the Black Down hills there is said to be an earth spirit nicknamed Charlie. He sits on the clavey or beam above the fireplace in houses, and is made of holman or holly.

One evening a farmer was giving a dinner party and he had once poured scorn on Charlie. Unluckily for him, Charlie remembered. When the guests assembled, they found the table bare, the silver put away and the tankards hung up and empty. All the food and drink had disappeared. This was a sure sign that Charlie did not approve. The dinner was cancelled.

Stogumber, a village in the Brendon Hills, is set in an agricultural area where hunting has been a favourite sport over the centuries since Cardinal Beaufort, at the time the wealthiest man in England, hunted here after the church was built in medieval times.

Combe Sydenham, two miles away, was the seat of the Sydenham family, one of whom married Sir Francis Drake. Legend claims that a meteorite, preserved there in the family home, and allegedly fired by Sir Francis from the Spanish Main, prevented his bride marrying a rival. Some think that if it is removed, it will always return.

◀ 'She noticed a man and a small
boy standing by the door . . .'

The white, ghostly figure of Sir George Sydenham—father of the bride—is said to ride down the combe every night between midnight and cockcrow on a headless grey horse, but it is the Wild Hunt who provide the most spectacular haunting as they ride through the streets with trotting horses, bridles a-jingle and baying hounds. When they rode through as late as the 1960s no one dared to look out as they heard the sounds!

Maybe they only wanted to drink at Harry Hill's Well. He was a leper said to have been cured there, and the sweet water from the well has helped other sufferers from many maladies.

Blue Ben was a fiery dragon who lived on Putsham Hill near Kilve. He used to get very hot—dragons do—and cooled himself by swimming in the nearby sea. To avoid the mudflats he came out from his tunnel below Kilve and built a causeway of rocks in the water.

'Each part of Somerset has its own
special aura and atmosphere . . .'

Then the Devil discovered Blue Ben's lair and used to harness him and ride him round the streets of Hell much to the fury of poor Ben who got very hot. One day, hurrying to cool after the Devil's ride, he slipped on the causeway and was drowned in the mud. A fossilised prehistoric creature was found in the last century near Glastonbury and said to be Blue Ben. He is thought to haunt his old seashore puffing with heat and rage in his efforts to reach the cool water.

Chilton Cantelo, named after the Cantilupe family, has an unusual, rather grisly relic in the form of a skull which refuses to be buried.

In life it belonged to a man called Theophilus Brome, a native of Warwickshire who came to Somerset to avoid the hostility of some he had opposed in the Civil War. He died in August 1670 and had requested that his skull be removed from his body and kept in the house, threatening a haunting if his wishes were not carried out. His body lies in Chilton Cantelo Church and his skull is kept in a cupboard at his home at Higher Chilton Farm. There it has remained.

Repeated attempts were made to bury the head but 'horrid noises' ensued throughout the house and spades were broken in pieces. The church was restored in the eighteenth century, and the tomb of Brome opened when a headless skeleton was revealed.

Some workmen emulating their Teutonic ancestors who were said to have drunk wine from the skulls of their dead enemies, drank beer from the relic evidently without hindrance.

The skull, when kept in a cupboard, remains silent, but beware those who disturb its peace after three hundred years. Brome certainly left a gruesome legacy in his home, but he is never likely to be forgotten.

In the last century a local ploughboy went to Rodhuish to have a plough blade mended. At the smithy, talk turned to the Croydon Hill Devil, a horned beast said to lurk in a lane over the hill. The butcher's boy thought he would scare the other lad by waylaying him and imitating the Devil. As the ploughboy approached the lane on his way home, a dreadful monster charged at him bellowing furiously. In his terror, he lashed out with the ploughblade and fled. All that was later found was a bullock's hide with a great gash in it and some horns, but the butcher boy was never seen again. It was believed the Devil had taken him. He can be heard howling on Croy-

73

74

don Hill on stormy nights when his and other lost souls are hounded by demons.

Minehead, a lovely seaside resort on the Bristol Channel's southern coast, is bounded on one side by the sea and at its rear by the thickly wooded steep and deep valleys of the northern fringes of Exmoor. Its harbour has been a haven for shipping over the centuries, and its situation in the shelter of towering North Hill ensures the protection from the strong coastal winds. But all has not always been plain sailing.

In the seventeenth century, Mrs Leakey was a woman beloved by all in Minehead. When she died her spirit underwent a terrible change, attacking travellers on lonely roads, conjuring up storms at sea and sinking ships, and everyone was in despair. Exorcism was tried but only made matters worse and provoked more violence. Charles I sent a Royal Commission to investigate, and at long last a bishop quelled the terrible phantom. Mrs Leakey's powers may have diminished, but beware of the Culver Cliffs where she is said to haunt still!

In the eighteenth century a prosperous innkeeper lived in Shepton Mallet by the name of Giles Cannard. He owed much of his wealth to dealings with smugglers, sheep stealers and highwaymen, and became involved in a plan to defraud the town of its common land. The news leaked out to the fury of the townsfolk who marched to his inn with murder in their hearts. Terrified, Giles hanged himself and was buried at the crossroads with a stake in his heart to prevent him from walking. All to no avail, and soon he was seen near his old inn—long since vanished—and near the crossroads where he was buried. There is a pub nearby called Cannard's Grave which had the sign of a corpse hanging from the gallows, its creaking making an eerie sound. One version claims that Cannard was the last man in England hanged for sheep stealing, but whichever is true, he is still restless.

Two other strange happenings are associated with this market town. In the dim past a hideous old crone, one Nancy Camel,

◀ '. . . a dreadful monster charged at him bellowing furiously.'

wandered the streets with her donkey cart. Then she suddenly disappeared without trace. Some claim she can be heard shuffling the streets at night, the hoofs of her faithful donkey clattering behind her.

In 1763 an invalid named Owen Parfitt, who had served in the American Army, was carried downstairs to sit in the fresh air outside his house. He was never heard of or seen again. Maybe the old woman took him away in her cart?

There are caves north of the town which are believed to bear the marks of an awful visitation by the Devil long years ago. There was a poor woman who lived in a cave. The Devil, seeing her poverty, offered her riches and a life of ease in exchange for her soul. She yielded to the temptation, but though she stayed in her cave she never lacked for anything and never had to work. She grew old. The time had come for her to fulfil her part of the bargain with Satan. The Devil came with a huge horse and cart to carry her to Hell. There was the sound of piercing yells and shrieks, and next day there was no trace of the old woman. The cave walls were marked with the imprint of a horse's hoofs and the tracks of a cart's wheels were visible. If one looks hard enough, they are still to be seen. And the poor woman still shrieks out for mercy.

Around the Quantocks are said to be many apparitions. At Weacombe a ghostly dog, evidently friendly, leads those who are lost to safety, and the road from St Audrie's Farm to Perry Farm has a Black Dog on its four mile stretch. No one thinks this one is friendly, and the area has other oddities in the shape of a coffin lying in the road and a 'grey, shapeless thing'. Maybe it has escaped from the coffin!

At Staple there is a belief that an old woman haunts the hills known as the 'Woman of the Mist' and a solicitor alleged she appeared to him carrying a bundle of sticks.

Stogursey has claim to both black dogs and witches. This village derives its name from the Norman family of De Courcey who had a castle which was destroyed during the Wars of the Roses. The

◀ 'A ghostly dog, evidently friendly, leads those who are lost to safety.'

church was originally a Benedictine priory and has some fantastic carvings. Nearby is Wick Barrow, once believed to be the burial place of Hubba, a Dane, but later proved to be a Bronze Age Barrow. Pixies have long been associated with the mound. A ploughman working nearby heard the sound of a child crying, complaining that it had broken its peel or wooden shovel for putting loaves in an oven. The ploughman found a tiny wooden peel, its handle broken. He thought the childish owner was hiding in some bushes and would return for its toy, so he mended it and left it where it had lain. When his ploughing was done, he returned to find the peel gone, and in its place a cake, hot from the pixie's oven. The child's cries can still be heard but no one else has had a cake.

Red-clothed fairies were said to have been last seen at Buckland St Mary where they were defeated in a pitched battle with the pixies. Afterwards the land was called Pixyland. The fairies' faint cries can be heard by those with good ears, and the pixies recognised by their red hair, pointed ears and preference for green!

In spite of long religious links and peaceful existence, a witch was supposed to live at Stogursey, who, if annoyed, would cast a spell powerful enough to overturn carts as they passed. And a large black dog casts a malevolent eye on people, often jumping out at them unawares. No one dares ask the name of his owner . . .

Muchelney Abbey, a Benedictine monastery standing on Somerset wetlands, must have given its pious inhabitants rheumatism, but the area also produced many eels so there was no shortage of food in Lent. The Abbey was Saxon in foundation and, though long gone, many of its stones are incorporated into other buildings nearby.

In its heyday, the abbey provided the setting for a sad, haunting tale. A penniless young man fell in love with the daughter of a wealthy knight who forbade their marriage. In desperation the luckless suitor became a monk and later Prior of Muchelney. There to his joy and surprise he found his love who, in her misery, had become a nun. Their love rekindled, they planned to elope, but were overheard and their secret betrayed. He was sent to a faraway monastery, but the poor nun, lurking in wait for her lover in a secret passage, was walled up alive. Her ghost is said to beg for release and his voice echo tɔ her from afar that he is coming.

Crewkerne and Chard lie in the south of the county towards the Dorset border with the Axe rippling below.

Crewkerne was known for its canvas trade and made much of the sailcloth for the fleet that sailed to defeat Napoleon. Present-day ships such as those sailed by Sir Francis Chichester and in the America's Cup yacht race were equipped with the same canvas.

Chard is an ancient town of Saxon origin, almost totally destroyed in a terrible fire in 1577, allowing for imaginative and attractive rebuilding. The cloth trade flourished here with gloves and lace as well, and its streams meander to the Bristol and English Channels.

Both places are busy, industrious and peaceful, yet the main road between them is said to be haunted by a phantom fight. Horses are heard galloping desperately and a fight witnessed between smugglers and Revenue men. A wounded Customs Officer can be heard gasping for breath.

The Westcountry has strong connections with the murder of Thomas à Becket as all four of the knights who killed him were from that area.

In a silent remote corner there is a lonely place which stands as a constant reminder of that martyrdom, for here are the remains of Woodspring Priory, once a religious establishment founded forty years after the murder by William de Courtenay, grandson of one of the perpetrators of the deed, Sir William de Tracy. He actually came from Devon and tried to sail to the Holy Land to expiate his crime. The people recited the rhyme, 'The Tracys, the Tracys, the wind in their faces!' to remind them, and fishermen were said to hear his voice wailing in the night winds.

Others believe that Reginald Fitzurse, born at Williton, founded the priory, and during the three hundred years of its existence, its land ownership was extended by gifts from the relatives of the murderers.

Two of the murdering knights were buried in unhallowed ground on the island of Flat Holm facing north according to legend. One of them, Sir William de Tracy, is said to utter cries of anguish as he tries to make bundles of sand bound with rope, and the curse laid on his family remains.

The ruins remain of an old infirmary erected in the nineteenth century as an isolation ward for sailors with cholera; it had a crematorium attached. In October 1900 the remains of a sailor believed to have died of bubonic plague were burned there.

Maybe his ghost lends song to the others in that lonely, eerie island. The priory still stands like a sentinel, silent witness to the past with an air of sadness and deep haunting.

Strange Sightings and Mystical Paths

ROSEMARY CLINCH

Rosemary Clinch has had a varied career in pub-
lishing with local newspapers and magazines
including editor of the Bristol Weekly Advertiser
and advertising manager and features writer for the
Bristol & West Country Illustrated. *She moved to*
book publishing specialising in local interest titles
and now runs her own successful business in
promoting book sales for local publishers, freelance
writing and undertaking research across a wide
variety of subjects. She is married and lives near
Bristol.

What was it a service engineer saw while he was driving his car down Chard High Street in 1975?

It was 8 a.m. on a February morning and no doubt reasonably light for the time of year, when suddenly his thoughts were interrupted. He caught sight of what resembled a huge bird with a wing span of twelve to fourteen feet. Passing briefly overhead it went out of sight over shops and houses in a matter of seconds.

No doubt he pondered on this experience for days.

What are UFOs? Are there such things as 'flying saucers' and ships shaped like long cigars containing smaller 'scout' vehicles? Are they really ice particles or space debris as scientists and astronomers explain or are they just clouds assuming strange shapes under certain weather conditions?

It could be said that to believe in ghosts is to accept something outside our physical world. But if we can accept visitors from the past, why not the future and why not outside our own solar system? Strange sightings go back to ancient times with reports of flying chariots, the sun dropping below the clouds, and 'magic' weapons of Celtic times when whole armies were wiped out by flames.

Legends tell of giants buried in long barrows and some say skele-

'There are accounts of factual sightings
of unexplained objects in the sky.'

tons eight feet or more have been found buried within them. Could
this be the reason many of them carry the name 'giant' such as
Giant's Grave at Holcombe and could they have been settlers here
from outer space?

Perhaps what our service engineer saw was one of the legendary
dragons. A dragon is said to fly between Cadbury Camp and Dole-
bury Hill near Clevedon guarding buried treasure. Strange clusters
of lights have also been seen on these hill-forts which connects with
the theory of UFOs being associated with ancient sites. Again can
one believe that legendary fairies could have been 'little green men'?
They too have been associated with ancient sites and round barrows
such as Fairy Toot in Somerset.

Intelligent and serious people seeking answers to the UFO
enigma have noted the similarity of the shape of barrows to the
objects sighted in our skies. These same people probably have very

little knowledge of archaeological terms but barrows have long been given the descriptive names of 'disc', 'bell' and 'saucer'. Reported sightings in recent years have more often consisted of shining silver discs, 'mother' ships, silver crosses and clusters of lights, very often moving at incredible speeds, faster than any aircraft made by man.

Misunderstandings often happen and although it can be said that scientists and astronomers do not generally believe in UFOs, they do keep an open mind. This is what a Weston-Super-Mare astronomer did when he was making his usual observations with binoculars one night. Suddenly, he saw a brilliant white light approaching him from the south at a phenomenal speed. Astonished, he watched it perform a sharp right-angle and double back on itself—at a speed no aircraft would be capable of.

Then it revealed itself for what it was—a white owl!

The astronomer's natural curiosity as to the reasons for this effect, found that this UFO appearance could be put down to the high sodium lighting content in that particular area of the town reflecting on the bird's feathers!

No so easily explained are one or two sightings experienced in the Bath area and reported in the local newspaper at the time. In 1982 in Bath, a salesman saw a large incandescent ball travelling slowly towards Box in Wiltshire at about 3,000 feet. He could only describe the object as totally alien and reported it to the RAF. No explanation ensued from this encounter but the Ministry of Defence took the matter seriously enough to ask him for a statement.

Again near Bath in Lower Weston a husband and wife were going to bed early one Sunday night in 1978 and, as they lay in bed facing the window, a tremendous orange glow came round the side of the curtain. Tentatively they watched as it was followed by an orange object shaped like a tear-drop lying on its side with a tapered tail. There was no sound as it moved very fast in fifteen seconds across the nightgathering sky, turning from orange to ordinary light.

Bath seems to have had a predominance of glowing orange sightings but one couple had an even closer encounter one evening between Bath and Melksham. They were following a ring of lights which they took to be planes flying in formation, but it was moving unusually slowly and their car eventually caught up. As they looked up underneath the object, they saw two rings of multi-coloured lights. There was no noise. It was a clear night and the object was 400 to 500 feet up and about 50 feet in diameter with its lights

Above: UFO sighting over Glastonbury Tor around 1977.
Left: An enlargement to give a close-up of the possible UFO.

slowly going on and off! A strange experience for what must be said were very sane and intelligent people.

There are many sightings recorded from reliable and in many cases ordinary people not wanting to appear they are from some 'crankish' lunatic fringe.

Many people in Somerset including a helicopter pilot at the Royal Naval Station in Yeovilton saw an orange disc which set off a spate of 999 calls from Aberdeen in Scotland to Wales in 1979. It was estimated to be travelling at about 1500 m.p.h. and, on investigation, Jodrell Bank reported it was certainly space debris.

To read Von Däniken's experiences and theories stirs the imagination despite many criticisms and accusations of misinterpretation, but the evidence for UFOs cannot easily be dismissed. Probably all of us have seen something in the skies which cannot be identified and yet casually ignored.

In 1953 George Adamski's book *Flying Saucers have Landed* created uproar in the realms of traditional science and intrigued millions. Both enthusiasts and sceptics had plenty of material to argue over, and they are still arguing.

In 1969 a distinguished physicist, Edward Condon, studied UFO reports going back twenty years held by the US Air Force and pronounced at the end of his findings that there was always a natural explanation for the objects seen. This was challenged by Astronomer Allen Hynek, Scientific Adviser to the US Air Force; the weight of respectability of reports from policemen, air traffic controllers and other experienced people, convinced him that objects seen cannot be explained away easily. An example is ball lightning which recent experiments have shown can exist but explanation is still difficult.

Perhaps the next 'Flap' as exponents of UFOs call times of regular sightings, will move in direction away from Warminster in Wiltshire, where in 1965 enthusiasts began to flock in their hundreds hoping to find evidence of visitors from space.

Unseen and even more obscure than UFOs in their fascination are ley lines, marked only for the 'ley hunter', by linking anything which is old and spiritually or otherwise sacred so that it forms a straight line on an ordnance survey map. There is a theory that UFOs possibly use these lines for navigation by tapping the magnetic power they are purported to contain. This is very difficult to prove but it is not difficult to prove the existence of lines which

Glastonbury Tor is to the 'ley hunter' a
main source for ley lines fanning in all directions.

appear to criss-cross the country from one ancient site to another.

Who was the originator of this theory? As a safe local dignitary in Herefordshire in the 1920s, Alfred Watkins was aware of the effect of any socially unacceptable theory. The archaeological world was outraged when, in his late sixties, he finally decided to reveal his findings while roaming through the countryside with leisured and retired members of a Naturalists Field Club, typical of many to be found in those days.

Megalithic man placed great importance on the way he positioned stone and had an obvious obsession with mathematics and geometry. But how did he do it, and is this again a possible link with UFOs and help from elsewhere? Could it be that since early man, and his possible use of these lines for spiritual power, their purpose has just simply been forgotten?

Leys pass through many such stones and some people have experienced sensations of shock or trembling when touching them, suggesting they are a power source. Identified by the name of the Living Rock are the fragments of an old megalith on the western slopes of Glastonbury Tor. It has been found these large fragments emit mild shock waves if touched early in the morning or late in the evening!

The mysticism of Glastonbury, with its reputation as a centre for a diverse range of religious customs and followings, is to the 'ley hunter' a main source for ley lines fanning out in all directions.

Glastonbury Abbey has the same geometrical plan as Stonehenge. Follow the line between the two and barrows, tumuli, earthworks, forts and churches can all be joined together.

Again, the Cathedral at Wells is directly connected to Glastonbury Abbey and stretches westward to Castle Neroch near Bridgwater. One of the oldest lines is the 'St Michael's Line' running from St Michael's Mount in Cornwall via Glastonbury Tor and the

One of the author's own Ley finds showing
Glastonbury Tor and Somerton as main connections.

remains of St Michael's Church and on to Avebury in Wiltshire.

Somerton also has a convergence of leys as well as Lamyatt at Lamyatt Beacon, the site of an ancient temple.

There is no overwhelming proof for the reasons why circles, tumuli and churches connect but the evidence is they do and it is hard to understand the reluctance of archaeologists to accept this. Anyone can prove it to themselves with a good straight ruler, well sharpened pencil and an ordnance survey map.

Just simply look for an ancient site, tump, cairn or fort. Look for other similar sites including churches, Roman forts, beacon points or holy wells. Crossroads, ancient castles, islands and ponds are all likely candidates—ring them all before taking the ruler to see if any of them connect.

It is surprising what one can learn about the countryside if prepared to run the risk of being called a 'dotty archaeologist'!

Megalithic Man's reshaping of our landscape with his movement of stones has a lot to answer for. Maybe we know how he dragged the Bluestones for Stonehenge from Prescelly but we still strive to understand his mind and his motives. Maybe legends and folklore have the answers, intangible though they may be, and perhaps there is more to be learned from the ancient art of dowsing.

The achievements of man 5,000 years ago were strange enough to have warranted the use of forces beyond the knowledge of man today and it can only remain to be said, 'There are more things in heaven and earth . . .'

One of the trees known as Gog and Magog. Tradition has it that they are two survivors from an oak grove going back to the time of Joseph of Arimathea at Glastonbury. ▶

Arthur — and Somerset?

MICHAEL WILLIAMS

A Cornishman, Michael Williams started full-time publishing in 1975. With his wife Sonia, he runs Bossiney Books from a cottage and converted barn in North Cornwall. They are literally cottage publishers specialising in Westcountry subjects by Westcountry authors. 1984 has seen the successful launching of their first Somerset titles, this coming in the wake of Legends of Somerset *and* Exmoor in the Old Days.

Was there really a King Arthur? Assuming he did live, was there a genuine link with Somerset?

Those two questions have fascinated, baffled scholars and searchers down the ages.

Here in the Westcountry one group of people, however, have no hesitation in answering 'Yes' in both cases. They are members of a psycho-expansion group run by Barney Camfield of Plymouth, a Natural Healing Therapist and Unitarian Minister.

They claim not only to have lived in Arthurian times, but some of them say they *were* Arthurian characters. The cynics will inevitably snort, but it might be worth reminding those critics that Dr Arthur Guirdham, a respected British physician, is convinced he is a reincarnated member of a thirteenth-century religious sect, about which he has written with considerable accuracy and detail.

Why not Barney Camfield's Arthurian set then?

The most extraordinary claim inside this group is that one member was, in fact, King Arthur. Moreover today she is a Westcountry

One of the Holy Thorn trees at Glastonbury. ▶

housewife with brown eyes. I have interviewed her twice: on the first occasion at her home in Devon and, more recently, at Land's End Cottage, St Teath, not far from Tintagel. Apart from being a mother, running a home, holding an interesting job in public relations, she still manages to find time to do healing and psycho-expansion—and to study astrology.

She started regression in 1979 and I asked her how it works.

'We relax into a state of heightened consciousness, the Alpha state. Briefly, the brain, as Colin Wilson has explained, has two halves: the left is the analytical side, while the right observes patterns and colours, and is intuitive. The tendency is to rely too much on the left in modern life. Generally, I believe, man is not realizing his full potential. Through this shift in the level of consciousness you become more aware, more perceptive rather like tuning into your own "mind computer".

'The discovery of my apparent life as Arthur, Artos, which is a very honest and real, albeit at times quite shattering experience to

'Glastonbury in the years running up to
500 AD had a very strong power . . .'

me, is only one of my many other apparent lives . . . some very ordinary and others extraordinary.

'I make no claims—I'm only willing to share a small portion, at the moment, of a happening which may help or be useful to others who are willing to search. I'm willing to say, however, that Arthur lives, and that the idea which this name engenders is only part of a mystery involving us all and, once begun, I feel the quest must continue.'

She sees nothing strange or inconsistent in the fact that once she was a man. 'Some people come back to this life many times,' she explained, 'and in very different forms . . . there seem to be no rules, save those of cause and effect.

'Today I'm an Aquarian, but then as Arthur I was Aries. That fits, of course—Aries, the first sign of the Zodiac, a natural for leadership.' She gesticulated with her hands, emphasising the now and the then. Her current Aquarian status fits too, in the sense that characteristic of this, the eleventh sign of the Zodiac, she is very involved in causes and service: a healer, a committed conservationist, and concerned in the welfare and future of society.

'Arthur had this great charisma. But he wasn't the chivalrous character that some of the story-tellers would have us believe. As a young man he was keen on women and fathered as many as fifteen children in various parts of Britain by various women.'

Within moments rather than minutes, she appeared to sink into a trance—the average layman watching her move from 'now' to 'then' would probably call it 'self-hypnosis'. In this condition her voice becomes noticeably lower in key, assuming an intensity that was not there earlier.

During both interviews I was forced to one of two conclusions: either this Aquarian lady was a convincing actress or I was watching and listening to something quite out of this world. At times, she appeared troubled, and at other times amused. Hers was no matter-of-fact commentary, no plateau of emotion or response to events.

Shortly after our first meeting, a Bossiney colleague asked: 'Do you really believe you have interviewed King Arthur?'

I found it a tough question to answer. 'I'm convinced the lady in question is convinced *she was Arthur*,' was my reply, and after our second interview that conviction was stronger. In between our two meetings she had subjected herself to a BBC Radio interview, though understandably had declined to reveal her identity.

In each interview she came out of a seemingly sleeping state gradually, just like someone awakening from a deep sleep or a dream, giving the impression of a weary traveller, arriving at a destination, or getting back. Barney Camfield describes the condition as 'relaxation of the mind . . . then comes what was termed by Goethe "contemplative perception". I don't know a better way to describe it.'

It was in our second conversation that we concentrated on the Somerset aspects of the Arthurian story. We talked on a wild March day, when rain and high winds swept across the landscape. Yet within a matter of moments, my visitor was back in another time and place. As soon as she had slipped into a state of psycho-expansion, I asked her: 'Did Arthur really have a Somerset link?'

'Now the thing to think of,' she said, 'is the whole of the south west peninsula, and that this man operated in that area . . . the link with Somerset is strong. I am pulled back there in the experiences I have to the Glastonbury area, and to south of that area, into Dorset in fact, which was where I believe I was born. But Glastonbury in the years running up to 500 AD had a very, very strong power, if you like, the earth power, a ley line, a meeting of leys and it looks like a grid if you were able to see it: grids of light . . . there are one or two very strong ones which go running right through the Tor. The present day you can still feel them but they are overlaid with many other centuries of happenings.

'If you get up on top of the Tor, (in fact in this life I have not yet been to the top, only in the experience of just running up to 500 AD) I can tell you what the view was like then. I would be really interested to get up out of these layers, because the higher you climb, the less influence of other centuries there are. However, a lot of people have been up there, and that Tor is not looking the same now as it did then. It is exceedingly different. It has had a portion taken off the top, and there was a temple built on the top of that Tor, and it was in the manner of a Greek temple, but it was circular. Within it was the most beautiful mosaic type of floor, and it was set in the manner of the Zodiac.

'And I had an experience where it was like a film, of climbing up there with a band of people—there was something like a dozen—and we entered into it and there were twelve columns round it. It was

◀ 'They set me up on my birth sign . . . Aries.'

whitish in colour, the stone, and underneath, I didn't enter, but I knew there was a hidden vault underneath the top of the flooring if you understand me. I just know that the top was domed, and entering into it there were seven people and they were clothed, I think, in pale blue robes—specifically seven. However, they set me upon my birth sign—the section attributed to my birth sign—and when I was doing this exercise I wanted to know what that was, and it's not very clear when you are actually experiencing it as the person, so you have to do two things at once, you have to pull away and watch it sometimes, and go back into it. So there can be confusion and I wanted to get this quite right, and I understood the birth sign to be Aries. I checked that out by doing something else, and it still came up and I had the symbol of the Ram. It didn't look like those we see now, but I knew it was, so that was his birth sign.

'He was set upon that, standing, and in the centre of the Zodiac they set a very large red crystal, and these seven knelt or sat, holding hands and they were within the confines of the circle. A circle is in any event very protective, and it protects those that are within it, or dealing with it.

'They chanted, and I can't tell the ritual but they certainly went through a ritual of some sort and I saw a light strike the centre from the ceiling if you like, from the Heavens, strike the crystal and they opened up their circle or their hands to me when that happened, and that light hit me right in the chest area, and I saw it was like a bolt of lightning you would understand because it hit me as a piece of energy, and I fell over. I can only tell you that it was an electrical charge and I knew that I was lying on the ground, and my sister Morganna was leaning over me, and another one was at my head, another sister, and they were giving me healing, and bringing me around. Now the import of that particular experience I knew to be very necessary. It had been contrived because although this man was very powerful, he was very egotistical. The problem with this is that he was going to use his own judgment all the time, in matters of great import as far as defending his tribes. His intuition and clairvoyant powers had to be further enhanced, quickly, to match his physical strength and courage, in order to carry the day so to speak in the forthcoming battles.'

A Glastonbury well. ▶

96

In our earlier encounter, this lady had told me quite bluntly that many writers had got Arthur wrong. I therefore asked her to say something about Arthur's background.

'My mother, Arthur's mother, was very beautiful, with long golden hair,' she explained, 'very small and she came from Wales, on the borderline country. His father (and this is unbelievable) was a man who was the seventh son of a line of Celtic royalty, sited in southern Wales, and because he was the seventh son he had enormous magical "power", and this was the way it was going to be. It was just like a story, but this was the way it was. He didn't have a great deal to do with his father in the early years. His father was away. This is where another man took over the physical teaching of weaponry and so on. This boy, who was brought up for the greater part in Wiltshire in a Roman villa, was allowed to view battle, not allowed to take part, but to learn about strategy and to take in distance and the feel of the land. It was a theme dependent upon the success in using terrain to the best advantage.

'He could see into the distance where no other man could. He had great natural intuitive powers. He certainly had charisma, and watching him as a boy, he was very full of himself. I suppose he had to be so. The mother belongs to another tribe as it were . . . she wears a purple robe and around her middle is something metal, linked, like a gold sash if you like, but it is made of rivets. It is quite beautiful and she is very clever. She is refined and something of the refinement comes off in this child, though he is so big and strong . . . she has Roman ancestry. This is where it is. This is carried through. So he has Roman blood in him. There is a lot of intermarrying; so it has produced quite an interesting strain. Whether it is strong enough to stand up to attack? There aren't enough of them. That's the message that comes across. They were intent upon preserving what they had built up and because of the change of social structure, this is seemingly what they talk about. They have every so often during the year gatherings and they negotiated with each other—the tribal leaders, and there are not enough of them. This is why they have got to work together and the only help will come from France, it will come from Brittany and Ireland, southern Ireland. That's all.'

At this point I put another question.

'With regard to the Arthurian terrain, where does Cadbury come into this, or is that just a piece of legend?'

'No it's not. It is a very, very important place. I can "see" that this particular fortress was very important to Arthur because it was a link in his fortress chain. I can pick up this information by viewing the area from above, as if I were in an aircraft. What I "see" is that there is a particular ley line going from Glastonbury to Cadbury, and from Cadbury it links around right up to the Severn estuary, going across the river to the south-eastern tip of Wales and there is another centre there. If you can understand this—that travel was much easier if you used those ley lines. It was speedy to use all the energy flow and you got from A to B much better than if you were off it. So they were used for communication in all sorts of ways.

'Cadbury, as with Glastonbury, is very very old. It goes back to when the British Isles wasn't a group of islands—to the times as far back as one of the "floods". Through mine and others' experiences during psycho-expansion, we found that around the time between 3000 and 2500 BC everything was very different. There were seven major "centres" over the face of the earth after the "flood". Centres being centres of light, as if enormous power was coming from within the depths of the earth in one place, and spreading out as if in a series of webs, getting less and less powerful, nevertheless linking as one. One of those seven major centres was Glastonbury.'

Again I came back with another question.

'Now about Arthur's grave—where do you think Arthur was buried, or might have been buried?'

'The grave at Glastonbury is not Arthur's grave,' she said, 'but the nature of his death was very prolonged and very painful. Where he died is very different from where his bones were laid because he was transported before his death and his body was transported after the death, and he suffered enormous physical trouble during the death. He lasted for a very long time and kept going in and out of the body, and it was as if he was between Heaven and Earth, moving between the two, and he wouldn't let go. It was his fault and this is the nature of the man. He suffered greatly with a very bad wound to the leg, and prior to that to the shoulder, and so half of him was mortally wounded, and the other half wasn't and he was almost split in two and you see how he died hovering between the two because his physical body wished to stay and the other half of him didn't, and this is the problem. So he is in the company of very few—those seven, who took turns in keeping the vigil, and in a sense legend has some of it quite right.

'The background to the death was this enormous battle. Because he had a son, and the son was very like him in stature, slightly less tall . . . and he wanted to be in the position of his father, there was enormous jealousy. This battle took place in Wiltshire (long pause) no, not this last one, the one prior to that last one. And so intense were the images growing at that particular time that it was the bloodiest battle, and they took him from the place and carried him south. I couldn't know where it was as I was in the body, and he was in and out of consciousness.' She paused here, and told me afterwards that it was in order to 'view' the event rather than experience it. 'It was some twenty miles south of Glastonbury . . . quite some way, further than I thought, and the way they go is through an old valley and the place is heavily wooded with the most enormous trees, and the clue . . . ah! . . . follow the ley line from Glastonbury south west, that will find the area, and there are still woods along this path now, but no little consequence to ask what town they were at.

'There is an older encampment or it *was* there. It is marked now on a map as a castle or fortress, set on a crag within this forest. And there is a hidden place within, they are like caves, and it is approached by a path going around the crag. There was a trench built, it is a ditch and it has not been in use, and it is an old old fortress even in their time—the time I am dealing with now. It is in disuse so it is only known to a few this place, and they are going along following the ditch outline, then coming right along the crag as it were. Remember that there are trees all over, overshadowing this whole thing. The trees are in leaf, denoting the time of year for Arthur's death, and it is an *extraordinary* place.

'There are caves, a series of them, but there is a biggish entrance which is not quite on the top. It is underneath the rock, but there is an opening—a portion open to the sky. There is an area in front of this cave entrance which is cleared and there is a stone, a standing stone there. Is it still there now? If it is still there, if it is, it's lost in all the undergrowth or whatever and that stone is in line with Glastonbury. It isn't a huge stone—it doesn't have to be because of the height of the promontory. That's where they are. O.K. We go in then. It almost seems as though it is on the border of Somerset and Dorset.'

'Can you give us just a little more detail about your—Arthur's —death?'

'I can tell you what happened as he dies. He is moved in and out of his body very gradually, in order to get him accustomed to dying. This is why it is taking so much time, as I said previously he is not happy about leaving his body as he has had such power in it, so the death is very difficult. He won't let go and he is very lucky in a sense that he is being cared for and having these almost like exercises of moving in and out of his consciousness and is shifting to different levels. He doesn't really quite know what is going on. He is having a very curious dream and meeting those who he has not seen for some time, and one of them is the person who is the man who was very very close to him during his early years, and taught him how to fight. He comes, or the picture of him, comes, moving towards him, and the idea that he will be seeing him again, even though he died long ago, is bringing all this to his realisation. It seems so strange since he is so tuned to the fourth dimension that he is finding dying so difficult—what a stupid man. Odd—and he eventually goes up.

'I can tell you that the beam of his life is something of a purple nature. That's the sound of it, it is purply and that is how he goes out on that path of energy, and he is lifted out in order to help him. It is a healing sort of colour. And he moves up. He doesn't think that he is really out of the body when he is, though he looks back and there is an enormous sense of relief. Well fancy that!'

Perhaps inevitably our conversation came back to Glastonbury— and then surprisingly my interviewee took a glimpse into the future, a reminder that psycho-expansion claims not only to go back in time but forward too.

First the Glastonbury of Arthur's time: 'If anyone has been to Glastonbury Tor and stood on the top and I haven't in this life, but I am doing it now as Arthur, I look to the north and all I can see for the most part are trees. Then I can see a clearing like an estuary in the far distance. I look to the east to the ridge, running south east. There is a ridge of country standing up, but again it's trees. Now to the south: beyond me there seems to be a hill which runs away into a marsh all around the southerly and south west side—it is marsh.

'There are channels for boats. There seems to be an almost guarding line of hills that way to the south and south west, and I look to the west and remember that seems to be the sloping side of the hill. On my right is this building which sprawls slightly at the bottom; there are some others almost like a little settlement and separate buildings . . . some of them seem to be supported by other

structures so that they are part on land and part on water. It is as though they are on stilts. No, they are not really on stilts, they are partly the basic structure of this settlement. It is completely surrounded by water, and this retains its purity so if you can imagine this white temple sitting on top of the tor and there are trees and rushes and water all the way round. It is very beautiful, and I can tell you; one of the things that is particular about the area is the scent. It's a most beautiful fragrant area—just being on that islet is restorative in itself. One is drawn there. It is what a pigeon would do; it would be homing in. No wonder it has still an intrigue about it. It's marked on time. I don't feel that it will come into an area of prominence again but I think it will retain something.

'What I think about the future—and I have seen this—is that water will come in again around that area from the north coast from the Bristol Channel and flooding will come in on the North Devon and North Somerset coast. It will be necessary in order to cleanse it—cleanse the land. It'll go again but it will be some time before it does, so we shall lose a lot of land, sometime after 2000 there will be a series of islands.'

◀'Water will come in again . . . It will
be necessary in order to cleanse the land.'

ALSO AVAILABLE

EXMOOR IN THE OLD DAYS

by Rosemary Anne Lauder. 147 old photographs.
The author perceptively shows that Exmoor is not only the most beautiful of our Westcountry moors but is also rich in history and character: a world of its own in fact.
'... contains scores of old photographs and picture postcards ... will provide a passport for many trips down memory lane...'   Bideford Gazette

LEGENDS OF SOMERSET

by Sally Jones. 65 photographs and drawings.
Sally Jones travels across rich legendary landscapes. Words, and drawings and photographs all combine to evoke a spirit of adventure.
'On the misty lands of the Somerset Plain—as Sally Jones makes clear—history, legends and fantasy are inextricably mixed.'   Dan Lees, The Western Daily Press

STRANGE STORIES FROM DEVON

by Rosemary Anne Lauder and Michael Williams. 46 photographs.
Strange shapes and places—strange characters—the man they couldn't hang, and a Salcombe mystery, the Lynmouth disaster and a mysterious house are only some of the strange stories.
'A riveting read.'   The Plymouth Times
'... well-written and carefully edited.'   Monica Wyatt, Teignmouth Post & Gazette

MY DEVON

Ten writers writing about their Devon: Hugh Caradon, Judy Chard, Andrew Cooper, Robin Davidson, Daniel Farson, Sarah Foot, Clive Gunnell, James Mildren, Mary and Hal Price.
'... ten writers' impressions of their favourite places ... the personal approach warms and enlivens...'   Herald Express

STRANGE HAPPENINGS IN CORNWALL

by Michael Williams. 35 photographs.
Strange shapes and strange characters; healing and life after death; reincarnation and Spiritualism; murders and mysteries are only some of the contents in this fascinating book.
'... this eerie Cornish collection'   David Foot, Western Daily Press

LEGENDS OF CORNWALL

by Sally Jones. 60 photographs and drawings.
Brilliantly illustrated with photographs and vivid drawings of legendary characters. A journey through the legendary sites of Cornwall, beginning at the Tamar and ending at Land's End.
'Highly readable and beautifully romantic...'   Desmond Lyons, Cornwall Courier